CREATIVE
HOMEOWNER®

AFFORDABLE
KITCHEN
Upgrades

CRE▲TIVE
HOMEOWNER®

AFFORDABLE
KITCHEN
Upgrades

Transform Your Kitchen on a Small Budget

Steve Cory
and
Diane Slavik

CREATIVE HOMEOWNER®, Upper Saddle River, New Jersey

AFFORDABLE KITCHEN UPGRADES

AUTHORS	Steve Cory, Diane Slavik
TECHNICAL ADVISOR	Joe Hansa
GRAPHIC DESIGNERS	Glee Barre, Scott Kraft
INDEXER	Sandi Schroeder, Schroeder Indexing Services
DIGITAL IMAGING SPECIALISTS	Fred Becker, Segundo Gutierrez

Manufactured in the United States of America

Current Printing (last digit)
10 9 8 7 6 5 4 3 2 1

Affordable Kitchen Upgrades
Library of Congress Control Number: 2011925582
ISBN-10: 1-58011-534-9
ISBN-13: 978-1-58011-534-6

CREATIVE HOMEOWNER®
A Division of Federal Marketing Corp.
24 Park Way
Upper Saddle River, NJ 07458
www.creativehomeowner.com

Safety

Although the methods in this book have been reviewed for safety, it is not possible to overstate the importance of using the safest methods you can. What follows are reminders—some do's and don'ts of work safety—to use along with your common sense.

- Always use caution, care, and good judgment when following the procedures described in this book.
- Always be sure that the electrical setup is safe, that no circuit is overloaded, and that all power tools and outlets are properly grounded. Do not use power tools in wet locations.
- Always read container labels on paints, solvents, and other products; provide ventilation; and observe all other warnings.
- Always read the manufacturer's instructions for using a tool, especially the warnings.
- Use hold-downs and push sticks whenever possible when working on a table saw. Avoid working short pieces if you can.
- Always remove the key from any drill chuck (portable or press) before starting the drill.
- Always pay deliberate attention to how a tool works so that you can avoid being injured.
- Always know the limitations of your tools. Do not try to force them to do what they were not designed to do.
- Always make sure that any adjustment is locked before proceeding. For example, always check the rip fence on a table saw or the bevel adjustment on a portable saw before starting to work.
- Always clamp small pieces to a bench or other work surface when using a power tool.
- Always wear the appropriate rubber gloves or work gloves when handling chemicals, moving or stacking lumber, working with concrete, or doing heavy construction.
- Always wear a disposable face mask when you create dust by sawing or sanding. Use a special filtering respirator when working with toxic substances and solvents.
- Always wear eye protection, especially when using power tools or striking metal on metal or concrete; a chip can fly off, for example, when chiseling concrete.
- Never work while wearing loose clothing, open cuffs, or jewelry; tie back long hair.

- Always be aware that there is seldom enough time for your body's reflexes to save you from injury from a power tool in a dangerous situation; everything happens too fast. Be alert!
- Always keep your hands away from the business ends of blades, cutters, and bits.
- Always hold a circular saw firmly, usually with both hands.
- Always use a drill with an auxiliary handle to control the torque when using large-size bits.
- Always check your local building codes when planning new construction. The codes are intended to protect public safety and should be observed to the letter.
- Never work with power tools when you are tired or when under the influence of alcohol or drugs.
- Never cut tiny pieces of wood or pipe using a power saw. When you need a small piece, saw it from a securely clamped longer piece.
- Never change a saw blade or a drill or router bit unless the power cord is unplugged. Do not depend on the switch being off. You might accidentally hit it.
- Never work in insufficient lighting.
- Never work with dull tools. Have them sharpened, or learn how to sharpen them yourself.
- Never use a power tool on a workpiece—large or small—that is not firmly supported.
- Never saw a workpiece that spans a large distance between horses without close support on each side of the cut; the piece can bend, closing on and jamming the blade, causing saw kickback.
- When sawing, never support a workpiece from underneath with your leg or other part of your body.
- Never carry sharp or pointed tools, such as utility knives, awls, or chisels, in your pocket. If you want to carry any of these tools, use a special-purpose tool belt that has leather pockets and holders.

Contents

Introduction

If you are reading this book, chances are you want to make improvements to your kitchen that fall somewhere between redecorating and remodeling. You've decided that there's no way you're going to tear out walls or remove and replace all of the cabinets and counters, but you're also looking to do more than just repaint the walls.

This book shows you how to work with your existing kitchen in small ways that will lead to large transformations in style and usability. In a kitchen, "making the best of what you have" doesn't have to mean settling for less than you want. If you choose four or five projects from the following pages, carefully select the best materials, and work patiently, you'll end up with a kitchen that is totally transformed.

As long as you're willing to roll up your sleeves and do the work yourself, most of the projects will cost less than $300, and only few of them will cost more than $1,500. The instructions in the book will guide you along the way. If you hire someone to do the work for you, you may need to double those prices, but that's still far less than a complete remodel will cost. And in most cases you won't lose the use of your kitchen for more than a day or two.

Redoing your kitchen one step at a time calls for some intensive work, but there's no reason it can't be fun. Enlist family members, at least in the selection process. Take a little extra time to do an especially careful job. Once you're finished, you can feel proud of your accomplishment as well as pleased with the results.

Weathered materials add character to a room and, in combination with painted surfaces, give a kitchen hand-made appeal, opposite.

A new coat of paint, together with a new sink, faucet, and backsplash, above, can brighten up the whole style and function of a kitchen.

The busy sink area is a focal point in most kitchens, right, and a good place to start a remodel. The details will really shine through.

1
Upgrade Possibilities

A full-scale kitchen remodeling is an expensive project. Fortunately, however, there are all sorts of ways to make a dramatic difference by changing one or two things. For example:

■ Refinished, refaced, or freshly painted cabinets, especially with new knobs and pulls, make a dramatic change to the look and feel of a kitchen.

■ New or resurfaced countertops and backsplashes can lend or add dignity or playfulness to the overall design.

■ A few new lights can make a kitchen more pleasant to work in and can add their own splash of style to perk up the kitchen.

■ Pullout shelving, pot racks, and other innovative storage solutions will help you organize your kitchen and make the most of the storage space, freeing up counter space and making cooking more pleasurable and less stressful.

The photos in this opening chapter may seem to show kitchens that are out of your budget, but most of what you see can be mimicked using techniques shown in the rest of the book.

Making It Your Own

Most of us are not designers. Ask any contractor, and he or she will tell you that the majority of customers ask to make changes after they've started installing a new dream kitchen. Making all of the decisions at the beginning can look fabulous on paper, but the lighting and other dynamics of your kitchen are different from the store model or the magazine photo that served as your inspiration, and even with sophisticated software, it's impossible to visualize how a total makeover will look until everything is in place. A one-project-at-a-time approach lets you live a while with each improvement and encourages tinkering with design and style concepts as you go along.

Consider the charm factor, too. Kitchens straight out of a store's showroom are a little like cookie-cutter houses: nice but just like what everybody else has. Most people like their home to have a special appeal, with unique features they've handpicked to create a style that expresses what they like. If you remodel your kitchen in a more gradual manner, you can take your time shopping around to find pieces that really work for you—pieces that make you smile when you look at them and that tie the room together. For some people this might mean adding special antique or "shabby chic" touches. For others, a few eccentric details like unusual handmade handles may cheer them up when they enter the kitchen with bleary eyes in the morning. Other homeowners might like to include tiles from exotic international locations. It can be fun to develop your kitchen's style around a few special and interesting details.

If you like the idea of creative kitchen upgrades with a personal touch and a design that you can test as you go along to be sure it feels and works well, this book can serve as a guide. Whatever it is you want to upgrade in your kitchen, be it cabinets, flooring, your sink or faucet, tiles, or lighting, this book will help you make it a reality.

Salvage yards and internet sources are good places to find unique items that to add personality to your kitchen. This cowboy pan rack, above, is sure to be a conversation piece.

Saltillo floor tiles, right, unify this bright Southwestern-theme kitchen; their reddish earth tones provide a mellow backdrop for the surprisingly bright reds and oranges of the countertop and shelves, and the blue accent tiles closely mimic the cabinets.

Over-the-top old-fashioned trim pieces, like a dentil detail on crown molding, above left, or a massive corbel to support a shelf, above right, can add a unique touch of style and class.

These iron-forged door pulls and knobs, below, have a rustic appeal that would work well with any type of cabinet, including modern.

Rustic details set the tone in this farmhouse-style kitchen. A salvaged piece of copper decorative trim (turning green with age) frames the backsplash behind the apron sink and wood countertop.

13

Eclecticism

Designers today are expanding the boundaries of style to create more colorful, interesting kitchens. Eclectic may sound like a euphemism for mismatched and disorganized, and it can be that. But a managed eclectic style can be fun and interesting. This might mean two contrasting styles or colors that bounce off each other—for instance, painted base cabinets and stained wood cabinets for the walls or for a side section of the kitchen. A managed eclectic approach opens up creative possibilities. The best designs often evolve, finding inspiration in early changes, to take the next bold and interesting step in developing a new and unique design.

You may have a fairly specific kitchen result in mind, but as you work toward that goal, it's nice to stand back from time to time and look at what you've got … and decide whether the next change you had planned is really the best move. It's a more considered strategy, and over time you can get a kitchen that's just right for your taste, your space, and your cooking needs.

Often the first move people want to make is removing an obvious eyesore—replacing an ugly sink and scratched counter or replacing a dingy floor or upgrading lighting. The removing-eyesores-one-at-a-time approach can be a good strategy. An eclectic design comes naturally with this approach, and so does a one-of-a-kind result. Once you remove one eyesore, you may find you have renewed hope that your kitchen will be nice enough to show off to company. Of course a new eyesore will probably emerge, presenting a new creative challenge, but you can then thoughtfully and affordably build on the work you've done to ratchet up your kitchen's overall look another notch.

White cabinets and yellow wall color are light and bright, above, but the design is more interesting because of the wood cabinets.Dark countertops add a zesty bit of definition.

With lots of natural light, opposite top, this kitchen glows with color. The design varies not just the cabinet colors but also the countertop surfaces. The walls and curtains in primary colors play off each other for a vibrant, lively effect.

The dominant color themes in this kitchen, opposite bottom, are muted green and the natural wood tones of the flooring. But the darker refinished wood cabinets and gray island surface make the kitchen more inviting and interesting.

Make Your Kitchen Work for You

Cramped counter space is a common kitchen problem. An open, spacious counter will improve the efficiency of your kitchen and make it look bigger and cleaner.

If you have numerous appliances on your counter—rice cooker, food processor, coffee pot— consider how you can modify your cabinets to take these often-used items off the counter while keeping them within easy reach. If you have cabinet space that's hard to reach, such as the space in a corner cabinet, consider how to make it work better; perhaps adding a lazy Susan or rollout features that make it easy to get at what's in back. A few well-chosen upgrades can make your cabinets and your whole kitchen feel much more organized and make the most of the space you have.

If you have space, you may want to add a few open shelves rather than new cabinet units. A kitchen that is completely covered in boxy cabinets may look tidy, but it also looks less open and airy. Open shelves add a little variety and style, as well as a sense of space and light, and make the overall design more interesting. You may even want to remove doors from existing cabinets to create open shelves.

Also consider freestanding storage units—for instance, a rolling pantry cabinet that you can move as needed to improve your kitchen's storage capacity and functioning. When company is over, it can serve as a beverage table; for multiple cooks, it provides another work surface; for everyday use, perhaps tuck it away in a corner to make the kitchen feel more spacious and simply use it for storage. To perk up the design scheme, consider buying or painting a freestanding storage unit in a color that contrasts with the rest of the kitchen.

This kitchen feels neat and organized, with all its nooks and crannies. Most of the cabinets and many of the drawers are open to view, making it easy to find things. Open shelves with baskets are inexpensive and always in style. Such easy accessibility is also ideal for homes with disabled family members.

Going Mobile

Portable table or shelf units are a welcome alternative to kitchen islands. Because the units take up less space, kitchens retain an open, spacious feel but have a valuable surface for food preparation or for someone to pull up a stool or chair to socialize. The table on the left has wheels. The movable drawer unit on the right is designed to be added on at the end of a counter, but it can be placed wherever you have need.

Creative cabinet storage features make it possible to tailor your kitchen's storage to your family's needs so that you can use and have easy access to every inch of space. Clockwise from above: swing-out shelves for a hard-to-reach area, an under-sink tote, a rollout tray that compactly holds cereal boxes, and a wide slide-out shelf unit for pots and pans.

Color and Style

A fresh coat of paint can do a lot to change the feel and personality of a kitchen, whether on the walls, the cabinets, or both. The tricky part is finding an overall balance for the whole room, taking into consideration wood tones, as well as flooring colors. If you have dark cabinets, you may want to add balance with a lighter color for walls and flooring; if your cabinets are light wood or painted white, on the other hand, you might want to provide some contrast. But anything goes. A lot depends on the lighting in your kitchen. Colors never look the same in your home as they do in the paint store, so take your time testing samples.

Kitchen walls are traditionally painted with semigloss paint because the shinier the paint, the better it resists stains and stands up to scrubbing. But today's improved paints (especially 100-percent acrylic) can be nearly as durable even in lower glosses, such as satin or eggshell. If you don't like the shiny look, consider stepping down the sheen a notch.

White-painted cabinets , above, are often a good choice for a small kitchen. Converting one unit to open shelves breaks up the monotony, and contrasting tiles on the floor and wall play off the colors of the wallpaper backsplash to liven things up. Bars with S-hooks provide hanging space for oft-used items and help maintain a spacious, open feel.

Cabinets that are refinished in natural wood should be protected with a scrubbable sealer like water-based polyurethane, left. The blues and greens in the wall and tile colors make the cabinets glow in this kitchen.

This eating nook just off the kitchen, opposite top, uses red and yellow shades of paint and fabric to create a warm, welcoming, and stylish restaurant-style booth.

The wood floor in this kitchen has been stained with alternating diamonds, for an argyle sweater effect, opposite bottom. This kitchen also has two types of cabinets and a darker wall color to accentuate the white ceiling beams and trim.

Mixing It Up

All-white or one-color kitchens are often featured in showrooms and magazines, and their gleaming clean surfaces are bright and appealing. People who feel that their kitchens are small or dark tend to gravitate toward this color scheme. And this may be a good choice for some homes. Over time, however, people tend to find this color scheme bland and tiresome. Current designer trends are mixing up colors and styles to offer— for instance, two types of cabinets, such as natural wood combined with painted cabinets, or two colors of countertop surfaces, such as a light-color granite combined with a darker granite. Increasingly, designers are combining styles, too—for instance, mixing retro hardware with modern cabinets or placing an antique piece of furniture at the end of a row of more modern cabinets. Again, the trick is finding an appealing balance; design rules are more flexible now than ever before.

Commercial floor tile in a checkerboard pattern is an inexpensive way to add splashes of color and pattern, left top. Here it is a great choice in a kitchen with no wood tones; a wood floor would look out of place. Notice how the rustic table feels at home with the clean white cabinets.

Black is not usually considered a cozy color, but when coupled with warm wood tones and splashes of color from dishes on display, it seems homey. In this design, left center, the black cabinets add an interesting definition to separate areas of the kitchen.

Cabinets in white and off-white contribute a subtle depth to the overall color scheme and provide a pleasant neutral palette that showcases splashes of color in the rest of the kitchen.

This kitchen, opposite, has a pleasant retro feel. The movable table in the center, though modern in design, feels right at home and offers more flexibility than a permanent island because it can be moved as needed, perhaps to occasionally serve as a buffet table for company. The open design of the table helps maintain a spacious feel in the kitchen.

Function and Design

Remodeling inexpensively usually means sticking with the basic space and configuration you currently have, rather than knocking out a wall or moving the sink or range to the other end of the room. If you want to add to the kitchen's functions — by adding a small desk for a computer for instance — you'll have to be creative when making it fit into the available space. This may require tradeoffs. But if you do some rearranging and make your kitchen storage space work-smart, you may find you can open up some space for adding an eating or office space.

Many cooks like to look up recipes on the Internet or watch recorded television shows to get recipes and tips from favorite chefs. To facilitate this, a simple under-mounted television or a reserved space for a laptop may suffice. A modest office desk with drawers can also provide a place for paying the bills. If you don't already have space for a desk, you may choose to remove a base cabinet and shorten a countertop.

A salvaged cabinet unit painted blue, above, adds a charming work surface and brightens up the decor.

An eating area just off the kitchen, above right, extends the use of cabinets by using short cabinets (designed to be installed above a refrigerator) as a base for a cozy bench. When you're using refinished wood in your design, cabinets don't need to match exactly: if they are made from the same type of wood, you can refinish them with the same stain and hardware, and they will look very similar.

Here, at right, a desk has drawers and doors that match the kitchen cabinets. To get the desk surface to the right height—30 inches—you may need to order special base cabinets or modify wall cabinets.

For a kitchen that needs storage space, especially for items used only occasionally, an extra row of cabinets that reach to the ceiling can add a lot of space without affecting the kitchen's layout. Here, opposite, matching glass cabinets showcase china, but it would also be possible to use cabinets in a contrasting color or with wood tones for the top units.

Details, Details

In a room so heavily used, details really shine through. Even a small upgrade, such as installing a new faucet or shelf, will have a noticeable visual impact and will subtly improve the morale of those who use the kitchen. If you find yourself feeling overwhelmed by all of the work your kitchen needs, pick a small project just to get the ball rolling. Start with whatever fits your budget or whatever you consider to be the biggest eyesore in your kitchen. There are many possibilities in this book, and we'll guide you through the process. Sometimes the hard part is just getting started.

Replacing base trim with something richer-looking is usually an inexpensive proposition in a kitchen, where only short sections of wall are visible. Special touches like this fluted molding, above, which protects the end of a wall, are available from cabinet makers and online sources.

A hot-water dispenser, below left, is easy to install onto most sinks, as long as you have an electrical outlet below. The dispenser makes it easy to brew tea, cook thin asparagus, and accomplish a host of other tasks that call for near-boiling water. Many styles are available, so you can probably match your faucet.

A small rolling unit with cutting-board top and wine and glass racks, below right, offers portable elegance.

A handy bookshelf, opposite, can be made by simply removing doors from a cabinet. You may choose to add bead board to the back for a stylish touch.

You can convert a 15- or 18-in. base cabinet into a wastebasket holder. This unit, above, holds two plastic containers, one for garbage and one for recyclables.

Plain cabinets can be dignified by adding small trim pieces, like the rope detail on the stained cabinet at right.

Tile Features

This backsplash, left, features handmade tiles that were a special find. They make a nice focal point over the cooktop surface in this kitchen. Even a set of four special tiles, right, can perk up the design of a tiled backsplash.

Partial Remodeling

Upgrading one feature at a time is a less challenging mental exercise than planning a total remodel. Some design decisions—say, which flooring will look best with the new countertop and refinished cabinets or which light fixtures will go best with a new color scheme—can be put off until later. However, don't neglect future decisions altogether. At least start thinking about projects down the road, even if you might change your mind later, to avoid painting yourself into a corner.

While many projects can be handled as solo enterprises, some need to be decided and installed in tandem. If you install a countertop, for instance, be sure to include the sink and faucet in your plans. You might simply reinstall the old sink, but you could be disappointed by the look of the old sink against the new top.

Design Tips for Partial Remodelers

- While you don't have to plan every design element ahead of time, you may want to determine a general direction. If you like "shabby chic," avoid gleaming modern light fixtures and perhaps go with a farmhouse sink and wood flooring. If you like a Euro look, aim for surfaces that gleam or recede visually and avoid natural wood that is too woody. If cottage style is your thing, stick to surfaces and fixtures with charming details.
- Go ahead and address what bugs you most, both visually and practically. If you have an ugly light fixture or a faucet that has seen better days, it's fine to start with those features. If you choose a fixture or feature that you really love, it will be easier to choose other elements to harmonize with it.
- Create personalized focal points that draw the eye. A stunning backsplash, for instance, can at least partially make up for cabinets and counters that are bland.
- Don't neglect the walls. Though kitchen walls are exposed only in a small area, their color makes a difference. Often, people don't notice the effect of bad wall colors until they repaint and see how much better things have become.
- Test, test, test. Things that look great in a store or photo may look completely different in your kitchen. Bring samples of countertop materials, and set them in place. Paint or refinish a cabinet door or two to be sure you will like the result. Set pieces of new flooring in place, and stand back to make sure they will harmonize with the rest of the kitchen. Look at these things at various times of the day and night because lighting changes dramatically in a kitchen.

Most of the elements shown here can be added discretely, with no more than a few days of kitchen disruption: backsplash, new coat of paint on cabinets, rimming sink, faucet, countertop, glassed cabinet doors. An island/table like this, left, could be made from a scavenged table that you might paint and cover with a wood countertop.

Open shelves and racks make a kitchen seem brighter and more spacious and make it easy to find things. For a quick kitchen face-lift: remove existing wall cabinets; paint the wall; and install units like this, right.

Have a Pleasant Remodel

By choosing to do small projects one at a time, you'll decrease the level of stress and anxiety that are the bane of a major rehab. In fact, with so much creative control over the details, you may find the experience satisfying and even enjoyable. Here are some suggestions to help you feel on top of the situation and tip the whole process in a positive direction.

- **Involve the family.** Keep everyone up to date about what's happening; if family members get a chance to offer feedback and to hear how the process will be affecting their lives, they'll feel included and will share your satisfaction when the project is completed. Remodeling projects can be teachable moments for the whole family. Though it's tricky to include children in the actual building process, taking advantage of their interest to let them help with a project can be a fun bonding experience—and a way for them to pick up a few basic skills appropriate for their age, like using a screwdriver or drill.
- **Keep things covered and protected.** Construction work always creates more mess and scratches than you expect. When painting, sanding, or doing anything else that creates spills and debris, completely cover nearby surfaces—cabinets, floors, countertops, appliances—with construction paper, a good canvas drop cloth, or plastic sheeting.

- **Minimize odors and dust.** Even latex paint has an unpleasant odor, and just a small amount of sanding can create dust that spreads like a cloud and insinuates itself inside cabinets and appliances. Do as much work as you can outside or in the garage. If possible, open a window and direct a box fan outward to expel fumes and dust.
- **Put some wiggle room in your schedule.** Allow ample time for U-turns, learning curves, and extra trips to the home-center store so that you don't get upset if things take longer than you expected. If in the middle of work you or your spouse are suddenly disappointed with a color or other design choice, take a deep breath brew up some coffee and make a leisurely decision. Remember that you will be living with your choice for a long time, so a few more hours of work now will be well worth it. Every once in a while, stand back and admire the fabulous changes that you are effecting in the most important room of your house.

If you don't already have a built-in oven, left, installing a new one can be complicated, so you may want to hire an electrician.

Granite-slab countertops, especially with an under-mounted sink, above, should be installed only by granite specialists.

Adding an island with a sink, opposite, is a project probably better left to pros because supply, drain, and vent pipes must be run under the floor. A professional-style range hood like this one may be installable by a capable do-it-yourselfer, as long as running the vent to the outside is not too complicated.

Working with Pros

If you choose to hire out some or all of the work, you won't have to come up with a complicated contract with incentives and penalties as you would for a full-on rehab. Most of the jobs will be of the one- to three-day variety. Still, you should take some time to establish the parameters of the work and perhaps produce a simple contract.

If you already have a handyman or contractor you trust, by all means call on him or her. However, just because someone is a good carpenter doesn't mean he or she will be a reliable electrician or plumber, so inquire as to whether he or she has have done the kind of work you are proposing. An electrician or plumber may charge more by the hour, but could cost less in the end because they carry all the supplies they need and can do the work more quickly.

For some small jobs that may have unforeseen complications, it's entirely appropriate to pay by the hour. For instance, installing slide-out shelves or refinishing cabinets might be easy or difficult; it's hard to know. But for flooring installation, tiling backsplashes, or replacing a dishwasher, it's appropriate to ask for a bid.

In general, the projects in this book will not require a permit or inspections from your local building department because there are no structural changes, new electrical cable or boxes, or new plumbing pipes. If you are at all in doubt, however, be sure to check with it.

2 Revitalizing Cabinets

A new set of good-looking cabinets for a medium-sized kitchen commonly costs $4,000 to $8,000 or more. But there are far less expensive ways to make yours look like new. These projects often call for more elbow grease than money for materials, but the time required is really not prohibitive: installing new hardware only takes an hour or so; adding a classy coat of attractive and easy-to-clean paint takes a day; sanding and applying a rich stained finish may span two or more weekends; and turning a plain door into a glass door occupies a couple of hours of your time. Complete refacing—installing new doors, drawer fronts, and veneer for the frames—is the most expensive project in the chapter, but it still costs far less than new cabinets. To see how to make your cabinets more functional by adding slide-out shelving and other storage options, see the next chapter.

Replacing Knobs, Pulls, and Hinges

This may be the quickest way to spruce up a kitchen. Even if you don't refinish your cabinets, new hardware can dignify and redefine their appearance. Many home centers have a good selection of hardware; or if you go online, the possibilities are nearly limitless.

If you choose pulls or knobs that can be installed using the same holes as the old ones and hinges that cover the same area as the old ones (even if the screw holes don't line up exactly), installing new hardware will take you only an hour or two for a medium-sized kitchen. Take old pulls and hinges with you when you shop for new ones so that you can accurately check whether the holes will line up.

If the new pulls or knobs require drilling new holes and filling in the old ones, the job will take longer. If you are painting or refinishing the cabinets, you will be filling holes anyway, so this won't be a lot of extra work. If the cabinets are being refinished, however, test to see how noticeable a filled hole will be after refinishing.

When installing new hardware in existing holes, take the old hardware to the store to make sure you get the right fit.

Installing New Knobs or Pulls

If you will install knobs or pulls where there were none or if you need to drill new holes for hardware, it's important to get the positions of the holes precisely correct. If a pull is even 1/16 inch lower or higher than a pull on an adjacent door, the difference will be noticeable. Make a simple jig that you can press against the door's corner for perfectly consistent hole spacing. (See page 34 for information on constructing the jig.)

Filling Holes

To fill and refinish a hole, use your finger or a putty knife to apply wood filler so it is slightly higher than the surface of the wood. Allow it to dry ❶; then sand ❷. Apply plain wood filler before staining or colored wood filler after the wood has been stained. Either way, the filler will be a solid color, so it will contrast slightly with the surrounding wood grain.

If the difference is apparent, try using a fine artist's brush to draw a stripe of wood stain to imitate the grain.

Use a drill with a screwdriver bit to remove the screws. A #2 Phillips bit fits most screw heads; for very small screws you may need a #1 bit. Antique hardware may use slot screws.

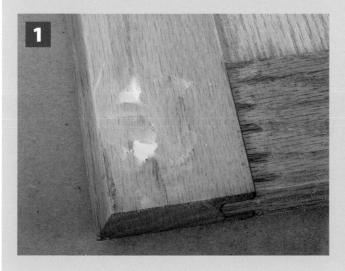

Installing Cabinet Hardware Using a Hole-Spacing Jig

• Measuring tape • Plywood and 1x2s for cutting jig • Drill with screwdriver bit • Door and drawer hardware

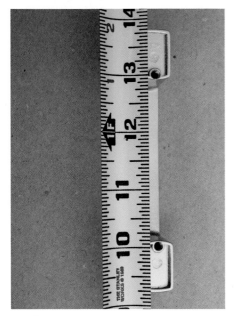

1 Measure to find the exact distance between the two screw holes.

2 Decide where you want the pulls to be installed, and measure for the positions of the holes in relation to the bottom and side of the doors.

3 On a scrap piece of ½- or ¾-inch plywood or stock, measure and mark for the hole locations. Use an awl or other sharp point to poke a starter hole in the precise locations; then insert the tip of a drill bit into the starter hole, and drill holes perfectly straight.

4 Attach pieces of 1x2 or other small lumber to the sides of the plywood to make a drilling jig. The 1x2 should overlap the plywood on both sides, so you can hold it against the door in both directions.

5 Test the jig on a scrap piece to make sure you end up with holes that are exactly correct. Hold the jig against the side and bottom of a door, and drill through the jig's holes to bore holes through the door.

6 Drive screws through the back of the door to attach the pull.

Euro-Style Hinges

Euro hinges are invisible once the door is closed, resulting in a clean and neat appearance. Most types have springs that close the door firmly to the frame, and they can be easily adjusted to move the doors slightly from side to side. They are surprisingly easy to install—as long as you buy a Forstner bit, which is made specifically for installing this type of hinge (below).

Drill the holes ❶ where recommended—usually, very close to the edge of the door and 2–3 inches from the top or bottom of the door. Drill pilot holes first; then drive screws to attach the hinge to the door ❷. Position the door in the frame, and drill pilot holes in the centers of the hinge holes (so you can adjust them up or down slightly), and drive screws to fasten the hinges to the frame. Once attached, the hinges can be easily adjusted to move the door side to side ❸.

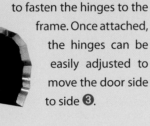

Refinishing Cabinets

If your wood-finish cabinets are in sound condition but you don't like the look of their wood tone, consider refinishing. This is a pretty time-intensive project. Depending on the wood species, the type of finish, and how elaborate the molding is, you may spend ½ to 1½ hours sanding and finishing each door and less time on each drawer face. If possible, test-sand and finish a similar door to get an idea of the time commitment.

For this project we show true refinishing, which calls for sanding down to the bare wood. You could apply "cabinet refinishing" products or a combination stain/sealer over doors that have been only lightly sanded so that most of the original finish remains. Results of this method can be attractive, but are more of a faux-finish effect than a true wood stain and finish.

As long as you don't mind living in a mismatched-looking kitchen for a while, you can take the job on in piecemeal fashion. However, plan to do the sanding and finishing in a workroom, garage, or outdoors to keep the dust and odor out of your home.

Here we show sanding to remove the existing finish and stain. You may choose instead to use liquid or paste strippers. In most cases, however, this takes longer than sanding—especially in the nooks and crannies, where the softened finish will collect. Sanding is a good deal less messy as well.

Removing a dark finish and replacing it with a lighter color, left, is a sure way to freshen up a kitchen.

Before applying a stain, top, test it on pieces of wood of the same species. See how they react to different light levels.

If cabinet doors contain glass panes, above, remove the glass before sanding and staining.

Refinishing Cabinets

• Random-orbit and detail sander with various grits of sandpaper • Lint-free rags and wood cleaner • Drill with screwdriver bit
• Angled foam hand sander • Razor scraper • Wood filler • Wood finish of your choice • Clear finish • Paintbrushes

1 Test small areas to make sure the cabinets can be successfully sanded. Some cabinet doors have solid wood trim around the edges, but the center panels consist of plywood covered by a hardwood veneer, which may disappear when you sand it.

2 Don't presume the stain you choose will look like the brochure pictures when you apply it to your cabinets. The actual color will depend on the type of wood and the top finish you choose to lay over the stain. Test stain-and-finish combinations on a door or on small pieces of wood of the same species.

3 Use a drill with a screwdriver bit to remove the hinges and drawer fronts (top). Clean all the surfaces to remove any oil and grime (bottom). Heavy-duty cleaner or mineral spirits will usually do the trick. Before you start to sand, test-scrape the surface with a putty knife to make sure you've removed all the grime.

4 Use a random-orbit sander to remove the finish. You could also use a simple vibrating sander, but a random-orbit sander, which rotates as it vibrates, is more effective at removing finishes. Because its edge is slightly flexible, it can be used on profile edges.

5 A triangular detail sander can reach most places the random-orbit sander misses. Press with medium pressure only, and move the sandpaper in the direction of the grain—otherwise, you could make scratch marks.

6 To get into the junction between the molding and the flat part of the door, if often helps to tilt the door up and run the detail sander along the edge of the molding. Make sure that the sandpaper does not dig into the flat area.

Continued on next page

Refinishing Cabinets, cont'd.

7 To get the last bit of stain and finish out of corners, you may need to use a razor blade too. Pull rather than push, so you scrape the surface rather than digging into the wood. Sand after scraping to remove any scratches.

8 If the corners look a little scratched-up, use an angled foam hand-sander to smooth things out. Apply only light pressure, and brush sand from the tool every so often.

9 Use the same power sanders to remove finish from the door frame. In most cases, you should sand only the parts that will be visible when the doors are closed—the stiles, rails, and side panels. (Sanding the inside of a cabinet would be time consuming and wasteful.)

13 Immediately apply stain to the rest of the surface. Aim for an even coat that is thick enough to stay wet for at least a few minutes. Finish by applying very light pressure and using long strokes that are in the direction of the grain.

14 The longer you allow the stain to sit, the darker the color will be. However, take care not to allow the stain to completely dry in any places. Use a clean, lint-free rag to thoroughly wipe away the excess stain. Always move in the direction of the grain, and aim at an even color throughout.

15 For a darker color, apply and wipe a second coat after the first has dried (top). If you end up with areas that appear lighter than others, wait for the stain to dry completely; then use an artist's brush to touch up the areas in need of darkening (bottom). Wait for five minutes; then wipe gently.

10 Remove all of the dust (very important); a tack cloth works well for this. Find a well-ventilated and dust-free environment for applying stain and finish; even small particles of dust will be visible to the astute observer of your finished work.

11 Wipe the wood with a damp cloth, and look closely at it: wetting will reveal any scratches or imperfectly sanded places. If you see problems, re-sand them now; they will be difficult to fix once you have applied the finish.

12 Apply stain (here, a gel stain) with a clean paintbrush, filling in the edges and corners first. Be sure to work the stain fully into all of the nooks and crannies.

16 Apply painter's tape as needed to keep from staining the cabinet shelves and walls. Apply stain to the cabinets in the same way as to the doors and drawer fronts.

17 If you applied a combination stain/sealer you can skip this step. If you applied stain only, allow it to dry completely; then apply a top coat of clear polyurethane, clear lacquer, or varnish. A water-based polyurethane is shown in the photo

18 Allow the stain and sealer a day or more to dry thoroughly. Reattach the doors and drawer fronts. Some top finishes (such as water-based poly) remain slightly tacky for a couple of days, especially if the air is humid, so advise family members to handle lightly.

Painting Cabinets

A fresh coat of paint will brighten up a kitchen in a hurry. As long as you have an ample dust-free space to lay out all of the doors and drawer fronts, painting cabinets for a medium-size kitchen should be a weekend project. You may, however, want to allow a few days for acrylic or latex paint or polyurethane finish to dry before reinstalling the doors and drawers.

Choose paint that is made to be touched and washed often. Oil- or alkyd-based paints give you the most scrubbable surface, but they are illegal in many states and produce fairly vile fumes during application. Paints specifically made for furniture or cabinets are a good bet, as are 100-percent acrylic paints. The glossier the sheen, the sturdier the surface will be, but high-gloss paint really emphasizes imperfections in wood. The most common choice is semigloss, but you may prefer a satin finish, which is nearly as durable.

Can I Paint Laminated Cabinets?

If your cabinets are covered with plastic laminate, they can be successfully painted, but be sure to take special precautions to ensure that the paint sticks. After cleaning the cabinets, power-sand them to scuff them up. Then apply an alcohol-based primer, also called white shellac. (The odor will be pretty strong, but will dissipate quickly.) After painting with acrylic paint, wait a week or so before handling the cabinets because the paint will dry more slowly than it would on wood surfaces.

Alternatively, clean and sand the cabinets; then apply a paint made especially for plastics. Do not apply primer first. You will need to wait a week for the paint to fully cure.

That All-Important Prep Work

There are three really good reasons to prep wood before painting:

■ To ensure the new paint will stick firmly. If paint is applied without adequate prep, it may peel in time—a real disaster that is difficult to fix. To be safe, clean the wood thoroughly; then perform two or more of the following: Sand thoroughly; apply deglosser; apply a coat of primer.

■ To block stains. Both wood stain and stains that result from cooking oils can bleed through paint, resulting in a blotchy appearance. Use a primer made with stain-blocking properties.

■ To smooth the surface. It's a mistake to think that paint will cover over bumps and holes; often paint actually accentuates these imperfections. Fill holes with wood putty or vinyl spackle, and sand them smooth, using power and hand sanders to knock down any raised areas.

For best results, use only top-quality paint for cabinets. Most homeowners chose a semigloss finish for surface toughness and ease of maintenance.

Drying the Paint

Acrylic or latex paint will dry to the touch quickly, but don't be fooled. It takes a very long time—months—for water-based paints to achieve full strength and scrubbability. If possible, let the cabinet pieces dry for at least several days before reassembling and using them. To speed up drying, run a fan in the room; even a slight breeze can greatly enhance the drying process.

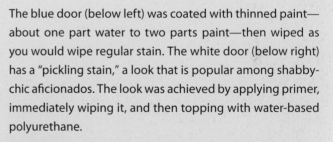

Is It Paint or Is It Stain?

A light coat of thinned paint can leave the wood's grain clearly visible, prompting you to wonder whether you have painted or stained it. Oak and other open-grained woods are easier to "stain" this way than woods like maple that have a less prominent grain. To open up the wood grain and make it more visible, wet the wood and allow it to dry just before painting.

The blue door (below left) was coated with thinned paint—about one part water to two parts paint—then wiped as you would wipe regular stain. The white door (below right) has a "pickling stain," a look that is popular among shabby-chic aficionados. The look was achieved by applying primer, immediately wiping it, and then topping with water-based polyurethane.

Painting Cabinets

• Drill with screwdriver bit • Sandpaper and hand sanding block • Paintbrush and roller • Primer and cabinet paint

1 Use a drill with a screwdriver bit to remove the doors and take off the hinges. If your drawers have screw-attached faces, remove the faces. If the drawer faces cannot be removed, remove the entire drawers and set them upright so that you can paint the faces.

2 Scrub with a heavy-duty degreaser or with mineral spirits until the surface is clean. Then use a hand sanding block with 100-grit paper to rough up the surface and give the paint something to cling to.

3 Fold a piece of sandpaper, use it to get into the joints and crannies. Periodically refold the paper when it loses its sanding power. Be sure that all areas are roughed up.

7 You may choose to brush the entire door, but a roller is a bit easier to use. A trim roller like this one produces a fairly smooth surface. If you choose to have a rolled flat area and a brushed molding, work the roller up against the moldings; then use the brush again to smooth out the moldings.

8 Paint the fronts of drawer faces; allow them to dry to the touch; then paint part of the back. Most of the back will not be visible.

9 Allow one side of the doors to dry to the touch. At this point they will still be tacky, so place the painted side on holdups like those shown before painting the backs.

4 Wipe the surface with a slightly damp cloth or a tack cloth to remove all dust. Feel with your hand to be sure that the surface is clean and smooth. Prepare a dust-free place to do your painting.

5 Apply a coat of stain-blocking-and-sealing primer. Use the same brush or roller as you plan to use for painting—any stipple you create can telegraph through the paint. Here we show applying white primer, but you can ask your paint dealer to tint your primer.

6 Use a brush to work the paint into any corners and edges. You may need to dab or push to ensure coverage of all the crannies. Finish with light, smooth strokes to remove any obvious brush lines.

10 Painting cabinet insides is a tedious job and should be avoided. Where a cabinet frame meets a wall, apply painter's tape to the wall (top). Stiles are usually painted with a brush because a roller cannot reach into the corners (bottom).

11 You may choose to remove middle shelves or apply small pieces of tape, as shown. Allow the paint to dry for at least an hour; then apply a second coat.

12 Allow the paint to dry fully; then reinstall the doors and drawer fronts. Examine the surface carefully, and apply touch-up paint as needed. If you used latex paint or finish, keep drawers and doors open for at least a few days with a fan blowing on them to minimize sticking.

Creating Glass Doors

If you have beautiful china, glassware, or collectibles to show off but don't want them to get dusty, glass doors are the perfect solution. It can be hard to find a glass door that matches your existing cabinetry, and if you do find one, it will probably be expensive. Fortunately, turning a plain door into a glass door is surprisingly easy in most cases.

In addition to plain glass, consider fancy glasses, such as seeded glass with scattered air droplets; glass with frosty etched patterns; or glass with molded patterns. These will cost more than the simple see-through variety but will add a stylish touch.

Doors with Molding. If the door has a decorative perimeter molding, cut partway through the door's thickness to make the glass opening, and use part of the molding to cover the glass. (See page 46.)

Plain Doors. If the door is a simple flat piece with no molding features, it is made either of plywood or solid wood. Either way, the basic procedure is the same: cut an opening; install trim on the front that overlaps the glass; set the glass against the back of the front trim; then trim out the back. (See Page 48.)

Cabinets outfitted with glass panels, above, allow you to display collectibles.

A combination of solid and glass doors, left, handle a kitchen's storage needs.

Frosted glass, below, lightens the look of cabinets that have a dark finish.

Well-placed cabinets with glass doors, opposite, become a focal point in the kitchen.

Adding Glass to a Door with Molding

• Molded cabinet door • Glass pane cut to fit • Measuring tape • Circular saw • Sharp chisel and hammer • Putty knife

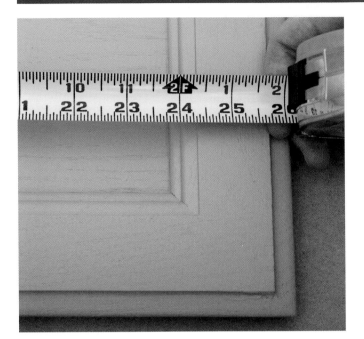

1 Measure for a piece of glass that will lap over the molding on the front of the door by a $1/2$ in. or so. Often, as in this photo, there is about $1/2$ in. of decorative trim on the inside of the molding pieces, which will cover the glass. In the case shown, you will cut the glass opening $24\frac{1}{4}$ in. long.

2 Buy a piece of glass $1/8$ in. shorter and narrower than the opening will be. Turn the door over, and position the glass so that it is precisely centered. You may need to first measure both sides and make marks on the back, to be sure that the front molding will cover the glass. Hold the glass in place with pieces of tape, and scribe a line around it.

5 Use a hammer and sharp chisel to finish the cuts at the corner.

6 Pry the pieces out. Part of the molding, as well as the center flat section (which may be plywood or solid wood) should pry out easily. If not, you may need to cut deeper.

• Caulk gun with adhesive caulk • Molding pieces for front and back • Finishing nails • Glazing points

3 Adjust a circular saw to cut about two-thirds of the way through the thickness of the door. Make sure it is not set so deep as to cut through the face. (If your initial cut is too shallow, you can always readjust and cut a bit deeper.)

4 Position the circular saw over a cut line. Retract the blade guard; turn on the saw; and slowly lower the blade to cut along the lines. Do not cut past the corners.

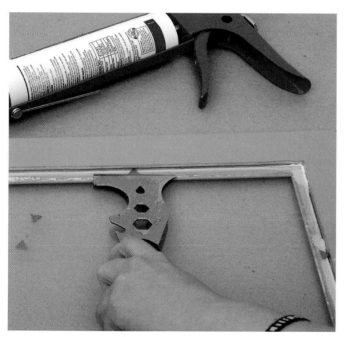

7 Use a caulk gun to lay a thin bead of adhesive caulk around the opening, and set the glass in the caulk. To hold the glass in place, press triangular glazing points into the wood.

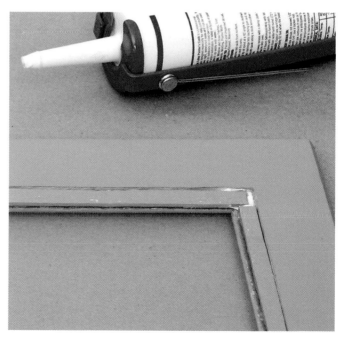

8 In this case, the pieces left over from cutting could be used to trim the back. You may need to buy other small trim pieces instead. Set the trim in adhesive caulk; fill the gaps with caulk or wood filler; and paint or finish.

Adding Glass to Plain Doors

• Plain cabinet door • Glass pane cut to fit • Pencil and tape • Drill with bit • Saber saw • Miter saw • Hammer • Caulk gun with adhesive caulk • Trim pieces for front and back • Brad nails

1 Remove the door from the cabinet. If you want the frame around the glass to be 2 in. wide, buy a pane of glass that is 4 in. shorter and narrower than the door. Position the glass exactly centered on the front of the door, and use pieces of tape to hold it in place as you mark for the glass's perimeter

2 Remove the tape, and finish drawing the lines; then remove the glass. Set the door on boards wide enough so that you will be able to cut with a saber saw. On the inside of each marked corner, drill a hole large enough for a saber saw blade.

3 Using a saber saw, cut along the outside of the marked lines (to make the opening about 1/8 in. wider and longer than the glass). Cut as precisely as you can, but if the cut line waves a bit, you can cover it with molding later.

4 For the front of the door, use a miter saw to cut pieces of molding (in this example, 1½-in. door stop) that will overlap to the inside of the cut opening at least ½ in. on all four sides.

5 Attach the molding to the face of the door using small brads and wood glue. If the trim pieces are very small and lap mostly (or entirely) onto the glass, attach them using adhesive caulk and no nails.

6 Set the glass in a bed of caulk, and secure it using glazing points, as shown on page 47, step 7. Use one or more small pieces of trim to finish the back of the door. On both the front and the back, set and fill the nailholes; sand smooth; and apply touch-up paint.

Removing Doors to Make Open Shelves

Open shelves are a nice complement to cabinets; they make the overall design more interesting and give you a chance to showcase things like colorful ceramics; of course, it's also more convenient to reach for things without having to open doors. One easy way to add a set of open shelves is to simply remove cabinet doors. (If you have a bare wall and want to install new open shelving, see the next chapter.)

To remove a cabinet door, simply unscrew the hinge screws. Fill the resulting holes with wood putty or spackle, and apply touch-up paint or stain. If the inside of the cabinet is not to your liking, you can paint it or cover it with a decorative finish such as bead-board. The shelves can be left as is or covered with shelf paper. Painting is also possible, but you will probably find yourself repainting every few years because plates and bowls will mar the surface.

Open shelves can relieve the dense feeling one gets from a bank of cabinets. You can remove the doors from standard cabinets or purchase open systems.

Refacing Cabinets

Refacing cabinets means replacing the doors and drawer fronts and covering the visible frames and sides with veneer. This gives you the look of totally new cabinets for a much lower cost than actual new cabinets. In many areas, cabinet refacing companies compete for your business. They will offer you a range of styles and colors from which to choose and can usually perform the entire installation in one day. You can save money by doing it yourself, as long as you have decent carpentry skills. Carefully measure your drawer fronts and doors, and order new ones from a home center or from an online source. The veneer may come with adhesive backing, or you may need to apply adhesive yourself. On a scrap piece of wood, practice applying veneer until you are able to achieve finished-looking edges. The trick for trimming is to hold the extra-sharp knife blade flat against the edge.

Proper Prep

Make sure that all surfaces are even and smooth, especially the transitions between stiles and rails, to get a professional-looking job. Use a block plane or sanding block to level uneven surfaces.

Refacing Cabinets

• Drill • Sanding block with sandpaper • New doors and

1 Clean the cabinets with degreaser or mineral spirits so that you do not see any gunk when you scrape it. Sand all surfaces to be covered using 120-grit sandpaper, and wipe off the dust. At a cabinet end, roughly cut a piece of veneer about 2 in. longer and wider than the cabinet end. Mask adjacent surfaces, and spray contact cement on the cabinet surface.

4 Make sure the veneer is positioned so that it will cover the sides when folded over. Press it into place, and roll it using a laminate roller. Use a utility knife, and cut the veneer so that it can be wrapped around the edges.

5 Fold the veneer around the stile so that the edges are completely covered, and roll it smooth using a laminate roller. Trim off excess veneer with a utility knife and a straightedge.

drawer fronts • Wood veneer to match the doors • Contact cement • Laminate roller • Utility knife • Clear polyurethane or other finish

2 Spray contact cement on the back of the laminate, and allow it to dry until tacky. Working carefully (as it's very hard to move the piece once it's stuck), lightly press the veneer into the contact cement so that it butts neatly against the wall and overhangs on all sides. Starting in the middle and working outward to remove any bubbles, use a laminate roller to smooth the panel. Trim the edges using a very sharp utility knife.

3 For covering the stiles and rails, use flexible veneer that has adhesive backing. Cut the piece to a width that covers the stile front and two side edges. Expose some of the adhesive at the top of the veneer; press it gently onto the stile; then pull off the rest of the protective paper.

6 Install flexible veneer on the rail in the same way as was done on the stiles. Use a square to cut it to length; test the fit; then press it against the rail. Wrap the top edge, and roll it smooth. Trim the bottom edge using a utility knife.

7 Once all of the veneer is applied, fill any voids between veneer pieces with wood putty that matches the veneer color. Apply a coat of clear polyurethane or other clear finish; allow it to dry; and install the doors and drawer fronts.

Replacing Drawer Glides

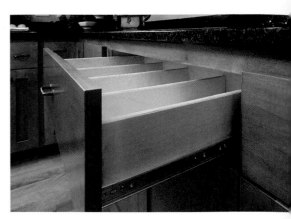

A cabinet drawer that sticks or wobbles is a common kitchen complaint. Sometimes the problem is that the original hardware was not meant to support a drawer filled with heavy objects. As long as the drawer itself is in sound condition, you can usually install new hardware—referred to as drawer glides, runners, or slides—that will make your drawer feel like new.

Here we'll show how to install two of the most-common drawer glides—side mounted and bottom mounted.

Many glides are rated according to the amount of weight they can support. Most kitchen drawers will do fine with a medium, or 60-pound, rating, but if you have a large drawer that will hold heavy pots, consider buying a set of heavy-duty glides that can support loads of 100 pounds.

This side-mounted glide can support drawer weights of up to 60 lbs.

Installing Side-Mounted Glides

• Drill • Small level (torpedo level) • Saber saw or keyhole saw • Replacement drawer glides • Strips of wood the correct thickness for your situation • Screws

1 Most glides require a ½-in. gap between the side of the drawer and the side of the cabinet opening on each side; in other words, the opening must be 1 in. wider than the width of the drawer. If you need to widen the opening, use a saber saw or a keyhole saw to cut the cabinet on each side.

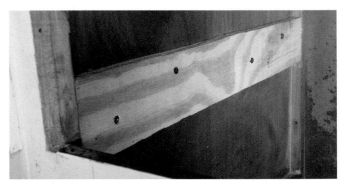

2 To make a cleat on each side, use plywood of the correct thickness, so it comes flush with the frame opening you just cut. Cut each cleat, 3 or 4 in. wide, and attach them to the sides of the cabinet.

3 Position the cabinet part of the glide so it is flush with the front of the cabinet frame. Check to be sure it is level, and drive screws to attach it to the cleat. Repeat for the other side.

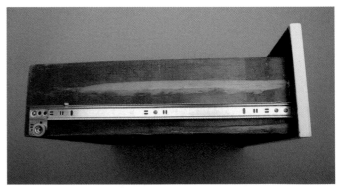

4 Attach the other part of the glide to each side of the drawer. For this type, the flange with the wheel should be flush with the bottom of the drawer at the rear, and the glide should be parallel with the bottom of the drawer. Guide the wheel into the cabinet portion of the glide.

Installing Bottom-Mounted Glides

• Drill - Small level (torpedo level) • Saber saw or keyhole saw • Replacement drawer glides • Strips of wood the correct thickness for your situation • Screws

1 Measure and mark a line down the exact center of the drawer bottom. Align the drawer part of the glide with the centerline running through the center of the screw holes. Drill pilot holes, taking care not to poke through, and drive screws to attach the glide.

2 Measure and mark the exact center of the opening, both at the cabinet frame in front and at the back of the cabinet. Place a small level on the cabinet part of the glide; check for level; and drive screws to attach to the front and back.

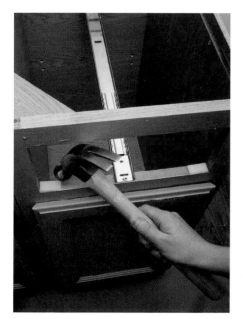

3 Attach the plastic guides to each side of the opening using nails. These support the sides of the drawer to keep it from wobbling.

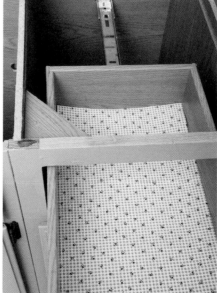

4 Insert the drawer's glide part into the cabinet's glide, and push. It may take a fair amount of pressure to fully engage the two parts.

Old Center-Track Hardware

TIP

Some older drawers have a center track inside the cabinet, into which a drawer-mounted roller is inserted; two plastic rollers on each side of the cabinet support the sides of the drawer. You can purchase replacement parts for this arrangement, and they will be easy to install as long as the center track has not come loose where it attaches to the rear of the cabinet. This hardware can support only light to medium loads and will not feel as solid as other options, but it is inexpensive and easy to install.

This type of hardware is often easier to install because you won't have to widen the opening. The bottom of the drawer should be at least ½ inch thick.

Crown Molding for Cabinets

If your wall cabinets do not reach the ceiling or a soffit at top, adding crown molding can add a special finishing touch that will make the whole kitchen look more dignified.

Crown molding can be made from simple one-piece stock or from a combination of molding pieces built up to create a fancier effect. Choose a profile style and size to match or complement the kitchen decor. The steps on these pages show a standard 3¼-inch colonial style, but you may prefer a smaller molding or something with a more modern look.

Crown molding can be confusing, but if you have basic carpentry skills, work carefully, and follow the instructions on these pages for cutting inside and outside corners, you should achieve success. Fortunately, installing crown molding on a cabinet is easier than installing on a ceiling because you can count on cabinets to be perfectly square.

Miter Saws. If you have a compound miter saw, which cuts at a bevel as well as an angle, you can lay the molding flat on the table and cut it. With a simple miter saw, things get a bit more complicated. You will cut the molding upside down; the side that rests on the saw's fence is the side that will be nailed to the cleats on the cabinet.

Great Installation

- Use a power miter saw or a high-quality hand miter box; a small wooden miter box will probably not get the job done.
- Buy extra molding stock because it's not unusual to make a mistake and have to start again.
- Look carefully at the molding, and identify the two back surfaces that are designed to lie flat against a wall and ceiling; they are at a 90 degree angle to each other. When you cut, hold these two surfaces firmly against the miter saw's table and fence.
- Clamp the molding firmly in the correct position to keep it from wandering as you cut.
- Don't attach the molding directly to the cabinet. Instead, nail some cleats to the top of the cabinet, set about ⅛ inch back from the front and sides, and attach the molding to the cleats.

Miter cuts at corners, left, are a sign of a professional-quality job.

Crown molding "finishes" any cabinet, opposite, that does not reach to the ceiling or a soffit.

Make Samples

TIP

It's very helpful to have samples like these, to use as reference when adjusting the saw for the real cuts. Cut the samples; then hold them in place at an inside or outside corner to make sure they are correct.

If your cabinets take a 45-degree turn (as often happens at a corner cabinet), make inside corner cuts that are 22½ degrees.

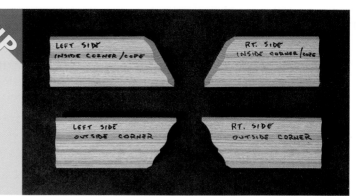

Cutting Crown Molding Using a Simple Miter Saw

• Power miter saw • Trim nail gun • Crown molding

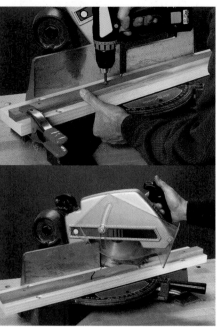

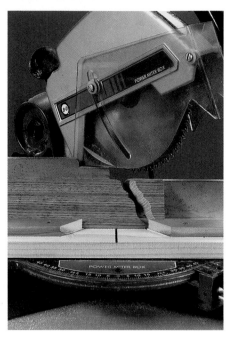

1 Make a positioning jig by cutting a straight strip as long as the miter-saw table. Position the strip so that it supports the molding against the fence at the proper angle.

2 Screw the support strip to the saw table. Keep the screws outside the range of the saw blade (top). Make cuts at 45 deg. left and right to cut through the strip; remove the portion between the cuts (bottom).

3 This is a simple miter-tsaw setup for a left-end outside miter (right-hand side of the joint).

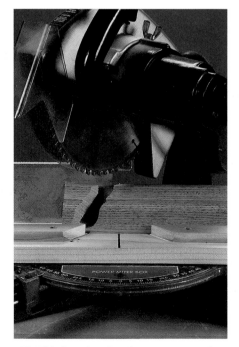

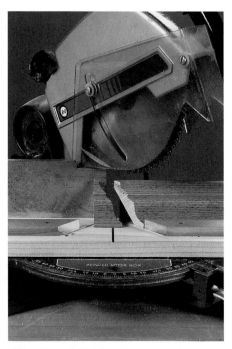

4 This is a simple miter-saw setup for a right-end outside miter (left side of the joint).

5 This is a simple miter-saw setup for a left-end inside miter (right-hand side of the joint).

6 This is a simple miter-saw setup for a right-end inside miter (left-hand side of the joint).

Making an Island

A kitchen island adds both counter and cabinet space that can greatly enhance a kitchen's functioning. Installing one is not as complicated as you may think: a basic island can be made using a base cabinet, a panel to cover its back, and a countertop. The countertop will likely need to be wider than the standard 25 inches.

First, make sure you have enough room for an island. Use a table or a piece of plywood on saw horses to simulate the future island; put it in place, and check that traffic will comfortably flow around it. If the space between your countertops on opposite walls is 7 feet or more, you likely have room for a modest island.

If you have extra space, you may choose to have the counter overhang the cabinet by 14 to 16 inches; this will allow people to pull up a stool and sit at the counter.

A "floating" island, below left, is simply an island on wheels. Many cabinetmakers sell these, so you can probably find one to match your other cabinetry. Most have a braking feature that allows them to spend most of their lives behaving as if they were a stationary island like those shown here (above left and below right).

Building an Island

• Base cabinet(s) with panel to finish the back, or special island cabinet • Straightedge or carpenter's square • 2x4 cleats

1 Determine the position of the island on the kitchen floor. Use a straightedge guide to draw an outline of the island. Check that the lines are parallel with nearby cabinets or walls. Draw a second line, inside the first, that indicates the inside surface of the cabinet.

2 Measure and cut 2x4 cleats to fit along the inside lines. Screw these down securely using 3-in. screws. If your floor is tiled, use a masonry bit to drill holes wider than the screws; then drive long screws through the holes.

5 Cut the plywood countertop base to size, and place it on the cabinets. Measure to see that it is centered. Using screws that will grab the plywood but not poke through, drive screws up through corner mounting blocks to secure the plywood.

6 If you will install tile on top, first install cement backer board over the plywood base. Or install a custom-made laminate, granite, or any other type of countertop.

• Countertop materials • Wood molding • Drill and screws • Construction adhesive and caulk gun • Power nailer or hammer with nails

3 Lower the island cabinets over the floor cleats, and check for square. Screw the bottom cabinet sides to the cleats.

4 Cover the back of the cabinets and any unfinished sides of the island with plywood veneer or a panel made by the cabinet manufacturer. Cut it to size, and install it using construction adhesive and finishing nails.

7 Install trim to cover exposed joints. Corner molding is a simple way to finish edges. You may choose to add base molding or base shoe to cover the joint where the cabinet meets the floor.

Add a Receptacle? TIP

Some codes require that an island be equipped with an electrical receptacle so that people are not tempted to string an extension cord across the floor. If the island will be used for eating, however, you may not need a receptacle. Electrical cable may be run from the basement below up into the cabinet; if you can't do that, you will need to run it through the floor. The receptacle is most often installed on the side of the cabinet.

Storage Possibilities

Standard-issue kitchen cabinets, which are basically large rectangular boxes, offer shelves and drawers to divide the space, but once they are full, seeing and reaching things in the back can become frustrating. Storage accessories help tailor cabinet and drawer configurations to meet your home's specific needs so that you can make the most of every inch of space and still have easy access. In this chapter, you'll find products that you can install in existing cabinets and drawers, including shelves and bins that slide or swing out and a variety of racks and hooks, and you'll learn how to build a few simple but attractive shelves. Most of the innovative products shown on these pages are available in different sizes and in a range of prices. By making a few upgrades to storage areas in your kitchen, you'll see a noticeable difference; your kitchen will look, feel, and be less cluttered and more organized; and it will be more inviting for the chefs in your family.

Drawer Organizers

The adage "a place for everything and everything in its place" is a good motto for kitchen drawers. If your drawers have a tendency toward chaos, a few well-chosen dividers can help authoritatively define spaces for small but important items that tend to go awry—perhaps your favorite knife, the pizza cutter, or the potato peeler. Most of the products you see on these two pages are adaptable to fit existing drawers. At most all you'll need to do is use a saw to cut an insert down to size.

Modifying a Cut-to-Fit Organizer

TIP

Some companies sell oversized drawer organizers that you can cut to fit. Use a table saw if you have one or a circular saw with a clamped straightedge as a guide. Cut the plywood flange upside down; it's less likely to chip that way.

A drawer near a work surface that holds both knives and a removable cutting board offers convenience and a clutter-free counter when the tools are not needed, above. This unit is a new drawer to which you attach the drawer face from your old drawer. A cheaper option is a knife-drawer insert, which you simply set into your existing drawer.

An expandable drop-in organizer like this at right can be adjusted to fit a variety of drawer sizes.

For a drawer with a little bit of depth, above, a two-tier insert can significantly boost storage capacity. The sliding top tray works well for frequently used items, and it lifts out for easy access to the bottom tray.

For oversize items that you need to keep handy, you can buy or make a diagonal drawer divider, above right. Long barbecue tools and ladles or spatulas fit nicely

This drawer divider, below, comes with a special section for storing and cutting plastic wrap to size, to make wrapping leftovers a pleasant experience.

If you remove the false drawer front by your sink, right, you can install a small storage tray that tilts open at a 45-degree angle to hold a few handy cleaning tools. (You then reattach the drawer front.) It's not much space, but it helps reduce sink clutter.

Stationary Cabinet Accessories

Shelves, dividers, and other stationary accessories make your cabinet space more organized and help lift clutter off the counter. As long as you order units that fit, they will be easy to install. Under-cabinet features add style and color as well as functionality. Railings with hooks, described on pages 80–81, can also be used under cabinets.

This under-cabinet spice rack, above, keeps the chef's favorite spices within reach. The unit matches the cabinets, but contrasting materials can also look nice.

A fold-down tray, above right, contains compartments for paper, pens, markers, and the like. Use it as a portable office for paying bills, making lists, and checking messages and emails. When finished, fold it up and out of sight.

If you have or would like to have a small bar area, a rack for hanging glasses, right, is a good idea to keep glasses at hand at all times.

This plate rack, above, actually sits on the counter, but if there is not enough space, it could be mounted under hanging cabinets. Use colorful plates to add a splash of color to liven up the kitchen's overall design.

A cookbook holder near the work surface keeps your counter space open for cooking and keeps your cookbook (or iPad) clean while holding it open at just the right reading height, above right. It neatly folds up when not needed and can also be used as a family message center.

Your paper towel roll, below, can look attractive if you choose a holder than harmonizes with your kitchen's cabinets. It's best placed off to the side of a work area so it won't interfere with under-cabinet lighting.

You can buy plastic-coated wire inserts to keep your cookie sheets and trays organized, or you can make your own more solid wood dividers, right. Use hardwood plywood, and perhaps cover the exposed edges with iron-on veneer. Nail on pieces of small molding such as base shoe or parting stop to hold them in place.

Back-of-Door Shelves

The space along the inside of cabinet doors can be useful for slim, lightweight storage. You don't want to put heavy items here because cabinet door hinges may have trouble handling the weight. But if you take advantage of this surface, you can add handy access for little things that you use a lot. For instance, a wall cabinet door near the range would be perfect for a rack holding your favorite spices. And near the sink, where you clean and chop vegetables, you might tuck away a cutting board. Under-sink cabinet doors can remove small cleaning items from the sink area, keeping them just as handy. It's all about minimizing clutter and clearing counters. The products shown on these pages are nearly as easy to install as hanging a picture.

This two-prong approach to storage—adjustable shelves and a lazy Susan—expand the use of this tall cabinet.

Installing Back-of-Door Shelves

Most cabinet doors are made of thin panels with thicker trim pieces around the perimeter. Be sure to drive any attaching screws into the thicker portion of the door. To install this back-of-door shelf, slide the flanges out and tighten screws to hold them in place ❶. Then attach the shelf by driving screws into the thick perimeter of the cabinet door ❷.

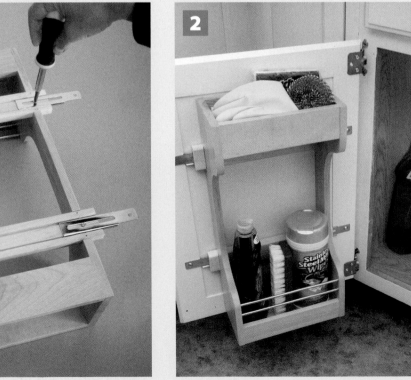

In a kitchen that's small or crowded, it makes sense to take advantage of any available space, left. Door-mounted shelf units are available in a variety of sizes and materials to fit any budget, and they are easy to install.

The slim surface inside a wall cabinet door, above, is just right for a small spice rack and keeps the chef's favorite spices front and center.

It's helpful to have the cutting board at your fingertips, but it's also nice to store it out of sight when it's not in use, below left. This attractive mounting rack is simple to install.

This handsome door unit for a base cabinet, below, takes your supply of crumpled grocery bags and makes them look neat and dignified. It also has a small tray on top for labels, pencils, or even a scrub pad.

Under-Sink Organizers

In many kitchens, the number-one ugly spot is the area under the sink. It's dark, damp, and dingy—and who wants to get down on hands and knees to find something tucked away in the back? Cleaning up this area will make you feel a lot better about your kitchen. Slide-out shelves and shelves that attach to doors keep everything off the cabinet floor and bring the dark recesses of the back corners of the cabinet into the light of day. Manufacturers offer a variety of products specifically for under the sink—ranging from simple, inexpensive plastic-coated metal racks to classy wood products that will make you want to show off your sink area to company. You will have to crawl under the sink to install some of the products shown on these pages, but the rewards will be worth it.

Under-sink shelving can be tailored to suit your preferences. Here, a tiered shelf in the back stores stock-up cleaning items.

Because of the plumbing lines, space is often limited in the cabinet under the sink. Make it more usable by placing items on a U-shape pullout shelf, above.

Supplement a cleaning-supply shelf with a small towel rack, above right, to put all cleaning equipment within easy reach.

Base cabinet doors are the natural place for cleaning supplies, but they can also be used for bulky food wrap and garbage bag boxes. Standing these items on end is a compact way to store them, center right.

Slide-out shelves under the sink make it easy to keep your cleaning supplies neatly organized. A lift-out caddy lets you carry the supplies where you need them, center far right.

Designed especially for under-sink base cabinets, right, this rubber mat is angled to direct liquids toward the front of the cabinet, so you'll know right away of a developing problem. The floor of a sink cabinet is often the biggest trouble spot in the kitchen.

Pullout Trash Bins

If your kitchen feels cluttered with containers for garbage and recycling, you might want to consider converting a base cabinet to a garbage center and installing slide-out shelves for receptacles. Manufacturers offer a variety of configurations to accommodate recycling programs, letting you separate trash into two, three, or four bins. Choose a unit that lets you easily lift out plastic receptacles for occasional cleaning.

Probably the most convenient location for garbage is near the sink and under a food preparation counter. This allows you to slide waste right into the container as you work. Pull-out units can accommodate up to four garbage containers, left, depending how big your household is and how much base cabinet space you have available.

Designed to fit inside 24-in. base cabinets, this recycling center, above, has three tall containers for plastic, glass, and metal and includes a canvas bag for paper.

This unit, below left, features a storage tray in the back to hold your supply of garbage bags. To attach this type of slide-out, first remove the door and fill the screw holes in the cabinet. Attach the sliding hardware much as you would for the types shown on page 52; then attach the door to the front of the unit.

Corner base cabinets are a storage challenge in terms of accessibility, and lazy Susans offer an elegant answer. Below, a revolving arrangement of garbage containers provides a lot of space for garbage and recyclables.

Attaching Trash Slide-Outs

Most trash slide-outs are easy to install. Measure the door opening, and buy a unit to fit. Place the sliding rack in the opening, and check that it is centered **❶**. Drive screws down through the holes and into the cabinet bottom to secure the unit **❷**. Now you can slide the unit out and add the garbage bin **❸**.

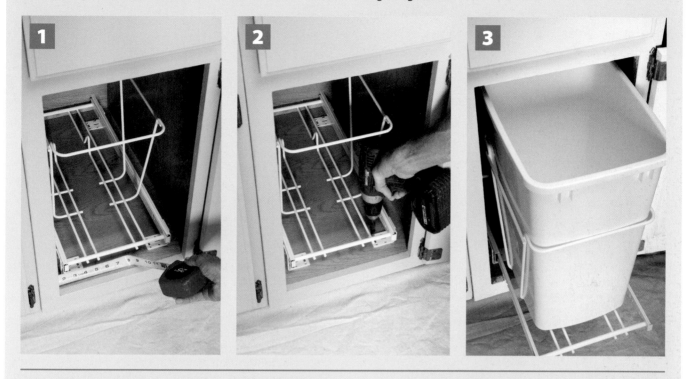

This type attaches in much the same way but is made with a plastic housing that can be easily removed for cleaning. Center the unit, and remove the little plastic plugs that cover the screw holes. Drive screws to attach the underlying metal sliding hardware **❶**; then replace the plugs, and snap on the front plastic housing piece **❷**.

Slide-Out Shelves for Base Cabinets

Many base cabinets have a door or pair of doors below a single drawer. The inside space behind the doors typically has two shelves; the upper shelf is usually only half-wide. This provides plenty of space, but you need to bend way over—and perhaps get on your knees—to get at pots, pans, lids, cookie sheets, and small appliances. Installing slide-out shelves puts all of these things in easy reach and saves your back and knees.

You can find some products at a home center, and more from online sources. Prices vary widely; wire units are generally less expensive than wood. Some units install by simply assembling them, then attaching them to the floor of the cabinet. Others, like the one at right, need to be attached at the sides and back as well. Measure the door opening, and buy a unit to fit.

Whether installed individually or as part of a two-tiered unit, pullout shelves put pots and lids in easy reach.

Basic Sliding Shelves

To install the most basic of sliding shelves you simply screw the sliding unit onto the floor of the cabinet ❶. Make sure that the unit is centered in the door and that it is at the right orientation to the front of the cabinet. Then simply insert the wheels of the shelf into the sliding unit, and push the shelf in ❷.

Blind Corners

If you have two base units that meet at right angles at a corner, there is an empty space—a blind corner in the back—that is unused unless a special shelving unit is installed. This fancy solution includes an L-shaped shelf that pulls out and pivots to provide access to the back of the back. The first shelf slides out as you open the cabinet door; then you pull and pivot it to reveal the blind shelf. Blind corner systems offer great accessibility, but they are pretty pricey compared with lazy Susans. Installation requires careful attention to manufacturers' instructions but no special skills.

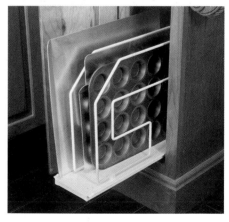

Keep pots and their lids organized in base cabinets, left, by placing them on pullout shelves. Page 74 shows how to install this kind of shelf.

A rollout tray, above, makes it easy to find the right cookie sheet without having to kneel down and flip through the tray contents.

Installing Two-Level Sliding Wire Shelves

• Sliding wire shelf unit • Measuring tape • Wood spacer • Screws • Drill-driver

1 Assemble the unit using screws. Test the height of the upper shelf to be sure it will easily hold lids and leave room for pots below. Adjust the upper strap to fit your cabinet depth.

2 Position the unit in the opening, and slide it up against the non-door side. Measure the distance between the door-side frame and the unit.

3 Cut a spacer ³/₄ in. wide and as thick as the measurement from Step 2. Slip it between the unit and the frame, and attach it using nails or screws.

4 Drive screws to attach the front of the unit to the frame on both sides. Also drive screws to attach it to the bottom of the cabinet, and to attach the upper arm to the rear of the cabinet.

5 Slide the racks into the frame, and test that they glide smoothly. You can now add sliding dividers, which simply squeeze into place.

Filler Units

Many base-cabinet pullout units have the door, and sometimes the drawer face also, attached, so instead of opening the door at an angle as usual, you pull it straight out. Manufacturers often refer to these as filler units. Once you slide it out, you can easily find what you're looking for, because you have a good view of the shelf contents from both sides and from the top.

A slim cabinet space, above left, is the perfect hideaway for a rack of spices, filling up a space that would otherwise be tricky to use.

One cabinet front conceals a number of pullout compartments, top, including a small cutting board.

Here's a sleek variation on the old pegboard method of suspending items on hooks, above left. Placing items in vertical position can be a more economical use of space. Plus, the handles are within easy reach, requiring no bending over to grab a needed pan.

Filler units often have two shelves that pull out separately, like this one, above right.

Perfect for oil and vinegar bottles and other liquid cooking elixirs, left, this unit would be nice to have right by the stove. But it is also able to accommodate 2-liter bottles for a pantry.

Pantries

A pantry can be defined as a storage area for food, rather than utensils. Whether you have a pantry area with tall cabinets or just want to maximize food storage in standard-size cabinets, you can find lots of shelving products to fit.

A built-in bread drawer, top left, has a sliding plastic lid to help maintain freshness.

Pantry base cabinets, top right, can hold a surprising amount of food.

A blind corner unit in the pantry, above, can nearly double what your cabinet unit will hold. See page 73 for more about blind units.

Filler units of pullout shelves eliminate the need to shuffle through everything in a cabinet to find a hidden can or jar, right. On this tall unit, up top, a stainless-steel pegboard neatly and compactly stores pots and utensils.

Utility Cabinets

Kitchens and pantries are such a central part of the home, if there is space, it's convenient to devote a cabinet to general family organizational needs.

This base cabinet, above left, keeps vegetables behind a closed cabinet door when not needed; wire baskets are an inexpensive pullout option.

A base cabinet with doors removed, above center, is a good place to keep root vegetables. These wicker baskets lined with plastic keep the potatoes in a dark place. Some manufacturers make baskets that slide out on railings, too.

If you use your pantry to store kitchen linens, shallow drawers like these, above right, will minimize wrinkles and keep your tablecloths and napkins looking freshly laundered.

This kitchen, below, has a base cabinet unit stocked with kid supplies, nicely accessible for short people. Clearly defined spaces make it easier to keep organized—in fact, it's not even possible to throw things in and shut the door!

Cabinet-Top Shelf

Adding a shelf with edge molding to the top of a cabinet will elevate the look of the cabinets and let you showcase some stylish pieces. A standard cabinet top is difficult to keep clean because it rests below the cabinet's frame; a shelf will be easy to wipe clean.

The shelf itself will not be visible (unless you are 7 feet tall or so), except perhaps for a very narrow reveal line between molding pieces, so you can make it out of plywood, or as shown here, medium-density fiberboard (MDF). Here we show trimming out with two basic, narrow molding pieces—chair rail below and cove at the top. You may choose other configurations—for instance, you could have a single piece of crown molding that covers the front edge of the shelf. Whichever you choose, be sure that the molding will not interfere with the cabinet door. You may need to raise the shelf up with a taller cleat.

The finished shelf can be painted the same color as the cabinet, painted a contrasting color, or stained and finished.

Adding a Top Shelf

• Plywood or MDF for shelf • Cleats and trim pieces of your choice

1 Attach cleats to raise the shelf, so the trimwork will be visible above the cabinet doors. Here we use simple 1x2s to raise it ³/₄ inch. If you have wider molding, you may need to use 2x2s. Cut the cleats to fit; drill pilot holes; and drive screws through them and into the cabinet frame.

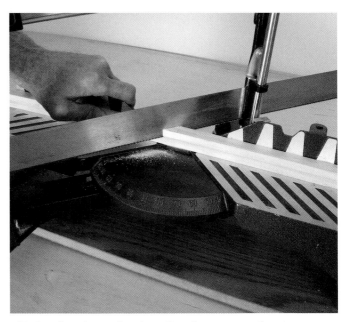

4 Cut the trimwork using a hand or power miter saw. Because cabinets are usually perfectly square, this is a straightforward cut.

• Table saw or circular saw • Power or hand miter saw • Nail gun or hammer with small trim nails • Wood glue

2 Hold a scrap piece of bottom trim in place, and measure for the shelf width and length. (In this example, the shelf will overhang the bottom trim by $\frac{1}{8}$ in. to provide another reveal line.) Cut the shelf using a table saw or circular saw.

3 Set the shelf on top of the cleats; do not nail it yet. Mark for cutting the bottom piece of trim. Whenever possible, hold the trim pieces in place and mark them rather than relying on a measuring tape.

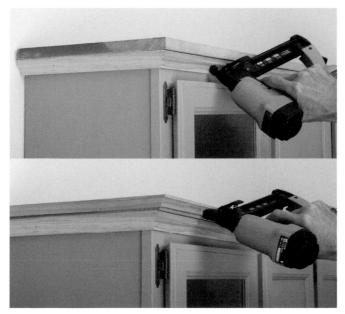

5 Nail the bottom pieces in place (top). If you don't have a nail gun, drill pilot holes and drive 3d finishing nails or trim-head screws. Adjust the position of the shelf so that it overhangs perfectly, and drive screws into the cleats to secure it. Cut and nail the top piece of trim so that it is flush with the top of the shelf (bottom). Set any nails that are protruding, and fill the holes with wood filler.

6 At the cabinet end there will likely be a gap between the bottom of the trimwork and the cabinet. Cut a very narrow piece of wood; squirt in a bit of wood glue; and slip in the wood spacer to fill the gap.

Rails and Hooks

Sleek railing systems with "S" hooks can suspend a variety of handy kitchen items wherever you have available wall space. It used to be common to see something like this for cooking utensils, but manufacturers have expanded the creative possibilities in recent years. The "S" hooks that attach to the railing can be removed or slid down the rail to a different position, offering a pleasant flexibility. Rails positioned under the counter or under an open shelf help lift clutter off the counter with style. These are as easy to install as a towel rack.

A rail system is ideal for small kitchens where counter space is at a premium. This kitchen uses railings both by the sink and on the end base cabinet. An under-cabinet shelf and a rolling utility cart help maximize storage space while still maintaining an open and spacious feel.

Hanging a Dish Rack

Some rail systems support dish racks and other accoutrements. Anchor the rail to the wall by driving screws into studs or by using heavy-duty drywall anchors ❶. Then hang the rack of your choice ❷.

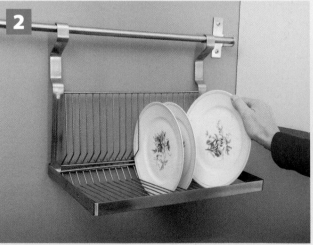

Eclecticism is both functional and attractive. Standard cabinets, glass-doors, and a hook-and-rail system, above, make a kitchen easy to use and give its design a lively feel.

A sleek stainless-steel rail system, above right, puts utensils in easy reach. A small rack just below an under-cabinet light holds recipe cards or a small cookbook.

A railing system is an opportunity to both clear the counter surface and add some color and style, below. It can be a good excuse to upgrade a few mundane kitchen items so that they will be fun to display and add some spice to the overall kitchen decor.

Put empty wall space to use by installing short racks for hanging pots and other equipment, right. If possible, place items close to where you will use them.

Lazy Susans

Lazy Susans have come a long way in recent years. There are several different shapes, including a curved blind-corner shelf that slides to bring back-of-the-cabinet items right out in front of you. There are lazy Susans for just about any cabinet, and the hardware that makes them glide is smoother than ever and often permits you to adjust the height of the shelves. These units are made to be installed into existing cabinets.

A lazy Susan is particularly useful in a corner base or wall cabinet with a face that is 45 degrees to the adjoining cabinets; it makes things much easier to reach than simple shelves. When buying a lazy Susan, measure not only the door opening but also the total inside depth of the cabinet; some older cabinets may be too shallow.

A specially hinged door, left, conceals a corner-cabinet lazy Susan.

This blind-corner lazy Susan, above, pulls out to give access to the back corner of the cabinet. See page 73 for more about blind corners.

A D-shape lazy Susan, below, makes maximum use of space in a corner cabinet with a 45-degree face.

Installing a Lazy Susan

• Lazy Susan unit • Drill-driver and bits • Screws • Screwdriver

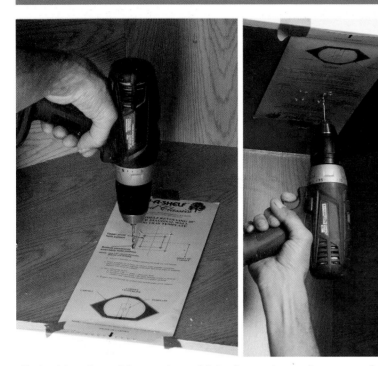

1 Position the unit's template with its front edge at the center of the opening at the bottom, and tape it in place. Drill pilot holes as directed (left). Repeat for the top of the cabinet (right).

2 Attach the top and bottom flanges by driving screws through the pilot holes.

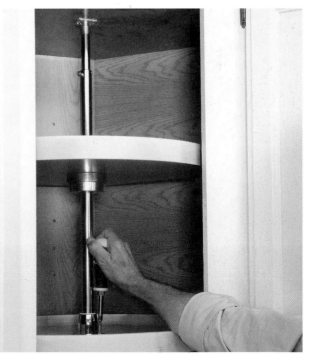

3 Assemble the hardware onto the lower and upper shelves. The bottom piece has rollers that allow the shelf to rotate smoothly; the upper part provides an opening for the pole.

4 Put the shelves into the cabinet; then slide the two-part pole through their flanges. Insert and attach the pole at top and bottom. Slide the upper shelf to the desired height, and tighten a setscrew to hold it in place.

Basic Wall Shelves

When it comes to open shelving, sometimes less is more. A straightforward set of shelves has classic lines that will look great in almost any kitchen. Depending on their contents, they can look rustic, elegant, or somewhere in between.

Shelf Material Options

Here we show building with medium-density fiberboard (MDF), which produces clean, straight lines and smooth surfaces. Be sure to cover all exposed ends with solid-wood framing or trimwork to minimize chipping. Also, cover your shelf unit with two or more good coats of paint.

Plywood is stronger than MDF, but less-expensive plywood sheets have noticeable grain on one or both sides. Cabinet-grade or hardwood plywood is a good choice, but it's expensive. Plywood should be stored in a flat position, or it may warp.

You may also use No. 2 lumber—1×8, 1×10, or 1×12 (which comes close to the depth of a standard wall cabinet). However, you may need to sort through quite a few boards to find enough straight ones. (If all of the boards in one store are warped, go to another store.) Unless you're after a rustic look, you will likely need to fill knotholes and sand rough spots.

If the shelves will be stained rather than painted, consider boards labeled "select" or "clear"; they are free (or nearly free) of knots. Oak, poplar, and other hardwoods are also good choices, though expensive.

How Strong, How Long?

TIP

Shelves that are too long for their strength may look great at first but will sag in time. How long can shelves be between supports? That depends on many factors, including the type and width of shelving material, the weight that they will bear, whether they are supported by plywood backing or not, and whether there is front molding or not.

In general, most shelving will be strong enough if it's attached to plywood backing and to vertical supports every 20 inches or less. To be safe, show your plans to a carpenter, or visit an online site that calculates shelf loads, such as http://www.woodbin.com/calcs/sagulator.htm.

Rather than stand out, simple shelves, above, recede and allow whatever is placed on them to be the focal point of the room.

Cabinet companies sell open shelving, left. You can mimic the look by building a shelf system and then adding moldings, side panels, and the like.

Choose a shelving system that suits the rest of the kitchen and the items the shelves will display, opposite.

Building Basic Wall Shelves

• Table saw and circular saw • Carpenter's square and angle square, pencil • MDF, plywood, or 1-bys for shelving
• Square-drive trim-head screws • Nails and wood glue • Wood filler • Putty knife

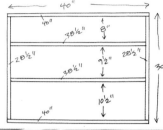

1 A plan drawing will help you determine the correct lengths of all the pieces in your shelf system (top). (The dimensions in red are the actual length of boards.) If you use a table saw, work with a helper and take care to keep the edge of the MDF against the fence all the time you are cutting (bottom).

2 You can also use a circular saw to make the cuts. If you use a circular saw, use a square as a guide. Work carefully; precise, square cuts will make the shelves look professional. Also cut the plywood for the back; it should be ⅛ in. shorter than the unit in both directions.

3 If you will paint the shelves, you'll thank yourself later if you prime—or even prime and paint—all or most of the pieces before assembly. You will need to at least touch up the paint after assembly, but painting now is much easier than after the unit is put together.

7 Holding the boards in alignment, drill pilot holes through the holes you made in Step 6 and into the side pieces. Then drive square-drive trim-head screws to fasten the pieces together. Check for square as you work.

8 Slide the two shelves into position, aligned with the layout lines from Step 5. Feel the front edges to check that they are all flush. (If the back edges are slightly unflush, it will not be as noticeable.) Drill pilot holes, and drive screws to attach.

9 Turn the unit upside-down, and lay the plywood back on it. The plywood should be slightly shy of the edges so that it will be invisible when the shelf is in position. Drive finishing nails every 3 in. into the sides and—very important for strength—into the inside shelves as well.

• ¼-inch plywood for backing • 1x2s for the frame • ¾-inch edging • Primer and paint • Drill-driver

4 Place the two side pieces side by side, and use a framing square to lay out the positions of the two shelves. Draw a line indicating the bottom of each shelf; make Xs that will be covered by the shelves. When figuring the distance between shelves, factor in the ¾-in. thickness of the shelves.

5 When working with MDF it's important to drive screws through the middle of its thickness and to drill pilot holes; otherwise, the material may bulge unattractively. Using an angle square to help, drill four pilot holes ⅜ in. from the ends of the top and bottom boards.

6 Set the top and side pieces on a flat surface to form the unit's box. Check that it is square at all corners.

10 Cut and attach the 1x2 frame pieces. Depending on your situation, you may choose to have them overhang the sides and top of the shelves by ⅛ in. on each side or cut them to fit exactly. Attach the top and side pieces, then the center vertical and attach using nails or screws.

11 Cover any exposed edges of MDF or plywood with screen mold or another ¾-in.-wide piece of trimwork. Apply glue; then drive small brad nails.

12 Fill nail or screw holes with wood filler. Allow it to dry; then sand it smooth. Paint the shelves; one coat of primer plus two coats of acrylic paint should do the job. Allow the paint to dry for a few days—preferably with a fan blowing gently on it—before attaching and placing items on the shelves.

Floating Shelves

Shelves with no visible means of support help break up the monotony of kitchen cabinets, adding some visual interest. Making them from scratch is possible but difficult: you need to drill perfectly level holes in the wall and insert dowels or metal rods into wall studs, then drill perfectly level holes in the shelf so that you can slide it onto the dowels.

Fortunately, you can buy floating shelf systems that include a wall-mounted bracket. These shelves are usually at least 1½ inches thick, to accommodate the bracket. Most units are prefinished, usually in black or white, but you can paint them to complement your decor.

Shelves with Brackets and Corbels

Installing shelves supported by brackets or corbels is a simple task. Use a stud finder to locate studs. The corbels may be screwed directly to studs, or they may come with mounting hardware that attaches to the studs; then you slide the corbel onto the bracket. Use a level, and work carefully; if the shelf is even slightly out of level, it can look sloppy.

A floating shelf seems to hang magically suspended. If properly attached, it can support a heavy load.

Installing Floating Shelves

• Stud finder • Floating shelf kit, with bracket and screws • Level and pencil • Drill-driver • Hammer

1 Determine the height and general location of the shelf. Use a stud finder to locate wall studs. If you have lath-and-plaster walls, use a special stud finder, or drill a series of exploratory holes (where they will be covered by the shelf) until you hit a stud.

2 Hold the bracket on the wall, with one screw hole over the center of a stud. Place a level on top. Once you are sure it is level, mark the positions of the other screw holes. If the bracket holes are not in convenient places, drill new holes. Drill slowly, adding drops of oil to keep the bit from overheating.

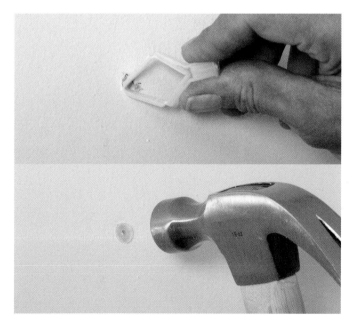

3 At least one screw should be driven into a stud—preferably more. If you cannot hit a stud and the shelf will not shoulder a heavy load, use plastic anchors (top). Drill a hole in the drywall or plaster; insert the anchor; and tap it flush with the wall (bottom). When you drive a screw into the anchor, the back of the anchor will expand behind the drywall to provide a fair amount of strength.

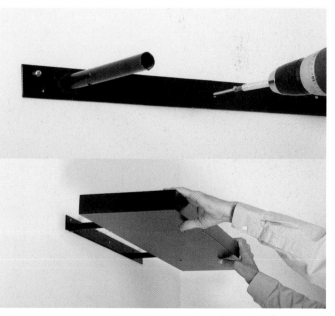

4 Drive screws to attach the bracket to the wall (top); then slide the shelf onto the bracket (bottom).

Pot-and-Pan Racks

Stacking pans on top of each other in a cabinet will sometimes result in an avalanche of pans crashing to the floor. Hanging them keeps them from getting scratched by their neighbors. If you have a good-looking set of pots and pans, this is a nice way to showcase it. Often placed over a kitchen island, a pot rack can go wherever it will look best in your kitchen. If people will walk under it, you'll need to adjust the hanging chains to get just the right height to accommodate foot traffic and yet make the pans reachable, or use a step stool. Pot racks can hold a lot of pans and clear out most of a base unit cabinet, so you can use it for other storage needs.

Many pot racks hang by four chains that are attached to ceiling hooks. Because all of those pots are heavy, the hooks are usually driven into joists. Attaching to joists will limit your location possibilities a bit. If that is a problem, you may consider using drywall anchors that are rated for 50 pounds or more; four of them may be strong enough—but there are no guarantees.

Wine Racks

A wine rack keeps your bottles organized. You can find ready made units that hang on the wall like a cabinet or rest on the floor like the one shown here. You can use a wine rack to make the unused space at the end of a cabinet run useful. If possible, keep the rack out of direct sunlight and as far away as possible from a heat source.

For a kitchen with low ceilings, a wall-mounted pot rack can be just as useful for clearing out valuable cabinet space. Chefs whose storage space is packed with pots may find that a unit like this gracefully handles the overflow. The shelf on top is a bonus for lids or cookbooks.

Hanging a Pot Rack

• Pot rack kit • Stud finer • Measuring tape • Pencil • Drill-driver • Locking pliers • Drywall anchors (if needed)

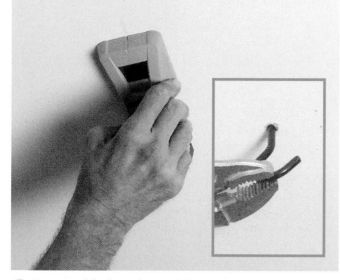

1 Use a stud finder to locate joists in the ceiling (top). In most—but not all—cases, joists will be 16 in. apart. Mark for the first two hooks; measure to see that they are equidistant from the nearest wall. At each hook location, drill a pilot hole and then screw in a hook by hand. When the going gets tough, use locking pliers or a long screwdriver to screw the hooks firmly up into the joists (inset).

2 Working with a helper, hold the rack in place next to the two hooks, and mark the ceiling for the locations of the other two hooks. Drill pilot holes, and drive those hooks as well.

3 To be safe, don't cut the chains to length yet. Hang the four chains at the estimated height, and attach the rack to the chains using the hooks provided. Test to see whether the rack is at a convenient height or not, and adjust as needed.

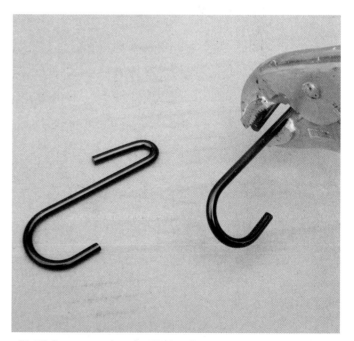

4 With many racks, the "S" hooks sit loosely on the runner, which means that they may come off when you remove a pan. If you don't like this, use a pair of locking pliers to squeeze the hooks so that they nestle somewhat tightly.

4

Backsplash Upgrades

A kitchen backsplash may be a single row of tiles or a piece of hardwood, often about 4 inches high, that protects the wall just above a countertop. In that case, the wall above it (and below the wall cabinets) is often simply painted or wallpapered. Often, however, people prefer to install backsplash tiles or panels that cover the entire space between countertop and wall cabinets. That's the kind of backsplash this chapter will emphasize.

A backsplash is typically only 18 inches tall and is partly hidden by wall cabinets, so in many kitchens its visual effect is minor. However, if you install great-looking tiles or sheet products, it can create a nice stripe of color and texture that can make your kitchen pop.

Backsplash Possibilities

Because backsplashes are relatively small areas, you may be able to splurge on high-end materials. You might even choose to create a design that reflects your artistic side—say, a mosaic pattern or picture made of tile shards.

The materials that you use for a backsplash should be easily cleanable because the backsplash is subject to food spatters. This is especially true for tiles installed near a sink or cooktop.

Self-Stick Tiles

Metallic tiles like this are easy to install: just remove the paper backing, and press them to the wall. However, don't get overconfident: because they cannot be slid into position once attached, it's important to get each one correctly positioned the first time.

The wall behind a range can become a focal point in the kitchen; it's an ideal place for combinations that add pop and break up the monotony. Here, subway tiles with bullnose trim neatly frame a section of mosaics that match the backsplash.

Prepping the Wall

Most kitchens have backsplash areas with smooth walls, and that's really all you need in order to install almost any type of tile or sheet. If you have wallpaper, you can tile over it as long as it is firmly affixed and is made of paper. Wallpaper made of vinyl or a rough burlap-like material should be stripped away first.

If the wall has small holes, you can usually tile over them; just scrape them first to make sure that the edges do not protrude outward. For a larger hole, scrape away any protrusions, and remove loose matter; then patch with a piece of drywall or a patching kit ❶. Apply joint compound; allow it to dry; then apply another coat, and sand it smooth ❷. Allow the compound to dry; then prime the patch ❸ to keep the unsealed compound from drawing moisture from the tile adhesive.

Sheet Backsplashes

Several manufacturers make sheets designed to be used as backsplashes. Styles and materials include plain and textured stainless steel, metal sheets with printed or embossed patterns, and PVC sheets in solid colors. The sheets can be simply glued to the wall using construction adhesive. You may choose to install small metal frames that fit around each piece.

Sheets like this can be purchased at home centers and furniture stores. They are usually about 3 feet long. If you want a more seamless look, contact a local metal fabricator, which can cut sheets of stainless steel to fit your space. It will help if you make cardboard templates of your walls. You can choose stainless steel that's shiny or a brushed or muted texture and sheen.

Brushed circular stainless-steel mosaic tiles, above, are an unusual but practical choice behind a range. Installation is straightforward, but the grouting must be done carefully.

This simple and elegant design, above right, features one neutral glass field tile with a thin band of glass mosaics to add spice. The tile and granite counter colors, all in one family, work together harmoniously. Notice how little cutting is needed by the window.

Mosaics that mix up the materials make the overall effect more interesting, below. Here small horizontal tiles in porcelain and glass juggle earth tones with brighter accents.

Honed travertine tiles that neatly match the color of the quartz countertop, right, are set in a subway pattern jazzed up with slivers of brown-glass "liner" tiles placed at each horizontal joint.

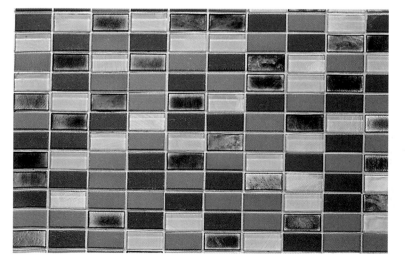

Mosaic-Tile Backsplash

A mosaic-tile surface has a rich texture composed of hundreds of small tiles. The range of design options is vast: individual tiles may be square, rectangular, octagonal, or other shapes. Tiles may be ceramic, glass, stone, or even metal, and may be all the same color, multicolored, or arranged in a pattern.

Mosaics usually come in sheets with mesh or paper backing. The backing holds them firmly in place, so they will not move out of alignment while you work.

The wall you cover with mosaics should be flat and even because small tiles will emphasize contours and bumps. Check by running a straight board or a level along its surface, and use joint compound to correct any obvious imperfections.

If you'd like to play around with a mosaic pattern, you can create your own sheets by installing individual tiles one at a time onto a large sheet of backer board cut to the size needed for your backsplash area. Allow the tiles to set; then use construction adhesive to attach the backer board to the wall.

The Right Mortar or Mastic

Thinset mortar is the usual choice for securing ceramic, stone, or glass tile. Use mortar that is "fortified" or "reinforced" with a powdered additive, or add latex liquid according to directions. For tiles that are translucent or light in color, use white thinset mortar; for other tiles, you can use gray.

On a wall where the tiles will not get soaked or bumped often, it's fine to use organic tile mastic instead of thinset mortar. This comes in buckets and needs no mixing; just scoop it out, and apply it to the wall. One advantage of mastic is that it is sure to be the right consistency; another is that it takes longer to set, so you have more time to adjust tile positions if need be.

Two tones of gray tile easily harmonize with stainless-steel utensils and cooktop, while the others provide just a hint of rust color.

Installing a Mosaic-Tile Backsplash

• Notched trowel of the recommended type • Margin trowel • Utility knife • Grout float • Mixing bucket and water bucket
• Mosaic tiles in sheets • Thinset mortar • Grout of a complementary color

1 Follow the mortar bag instructions, and mix the mortar in a bucket with water or latex additive. To ensure that all of the tiles adhere but that mortar does not squeeze out between the tiles, mix the thinset mortar to just the right consistency—not runny but not too dry. A margin trowel is the best tool for hand mixing.

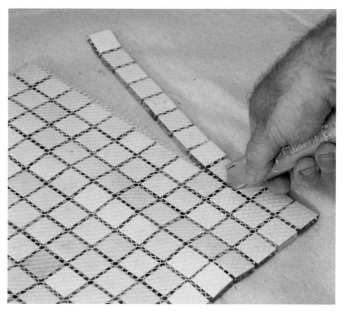

2 If the individual tiles are small, it is usually not practical to cut them to fit. Instead, just turn the sheet over, and cut the backing with a utility knife. (If this leaves a gap just below the cabinet, you can fill it with wood or grout, as seen in Step 11). If the tiles are fairly large, cut them using a snap cutter, a wet saw, or tile nippers.

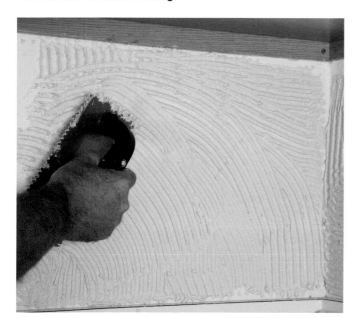

3 Do a test run, and cut several sheets to size. Using a notched trowel of the type recommended by the tile dealer, scoop mortar out of the bucket, and press it onto the wall. Comb with the notches lightly scraping against the wall. The trowel pattern does not have to be neat, but you should work to eliminate any globs or gaps.

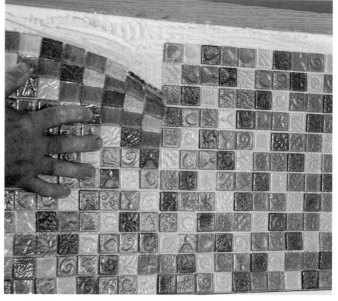

4 Gently press a sheet into the mortar, starting at the bottom and moving upward. The tiles on each sheet will be correctly spaced, but it's up to you to monitor the spacing between sheets to achieve a continuous pattern. Make sure that each sheet is perfectly placed before installing the next.

Continued on next page

Installing a Mosaic-Tile Backsplash, cont'd.

5 Press and tap the tiles using a straight 2x4 or 2x6 to make sure that they are all embedded in the mortar. Run the board across the surface to make sure it is smooth and even.

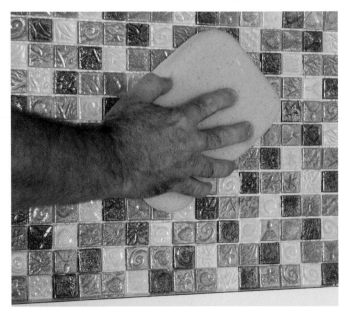

6 Once you've set several sheets, gently wipe the surface with a damp sponge to clean away any squeezed-out mortar. If a good deal of mortar is squeezing out, hold the trowel at a flatter angle when you install future tiles, so the mortar is not going on as thick.

9 Fill a large bucket with water. Dampen a sponge, and wipe gently to remove grout from the tile surface, leaving the grouted joints level at a height just slightly below the tile surface. You'll need to rinse the sponge often to keep it clean.

10 Allow the grout to partially dry, and wipe again one or two times. Look closely at the joints, and aim for a consistent depth and texture. If a gap in the grout appears, use your finger to fill it; then wipe gently. Allow several hours or more for the grout to fully dry; then use a dry cloth to buff the tiles until they shine.

7 Give the mortar a day or two to set. Use a margin trowel to mix a batch of grout in a bucket, aiming for the consistency of toothpaste or mayonnaise. Allow the grout to "slake" for 10 minutes or so; then remix it. Scoop out the grout using a grout float, and press it into the tile surface, holding the float nearly flat against the wall.

8 Press the grout into the joints by moving the float in several directions at all points. Then tilt the float up, and use it to squeegee away most of the grout on the surface of the tiles. Move the float at angles to the grout joints to avoid digging into the joints. If you see gaps, press grout into them, and scrape again.

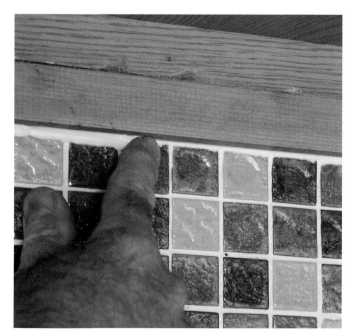

11 If there is a sizable gap below the cabinets or elsewhere that is too narrow for a row of tiles, rip a piece of wood to fill it, and caulk the joint between the tiles and the wood.

Choosing Grout

If the gap between tiles is 1/8 inch or less, use unsanded grout; if it is greater than 1/8 inch, use sanded grout. Choose grout that is latex or polymer fortified, or add liquid latex when you mix it; unfortified grout will crack over time.

A home center or tile dealer will have a selection of small grout samples, below, that you can hold up against the tiles to choose grout color. Avoid the temptation to choose a dark or contrasting grout color to add visual interest; this will really highlight imperfections in tile spacing. As much as possible, choose a color that comes close to a color in the tiles.

Slate or Other Rough Stone Backsplashes

Rustic-looking tiles with earth tones in swirled or blotchy patterns make a handsome backdrop for food-prep areas. Tiles like these can often be found on sale for very low prices, either at a home center or a tile store.

Examine the tiles to make sure they will suit your decor and to understand how you will install them. Because these tiles are natural stone, color may vary greatly, so one box of tiles may look different from another. Some slate tiles are cut precisely and are perfectly flat with straight edges and square corners. Rougher types often have edges that are not straight, and they may vary considerably in thickness. To install these more rustic tiles, you will need to work slowly, adding extra mortar to make the thinner tiles come out to the same surface as the thicker ones. Or you can opt for an uneven surface to emphasize the rustic effect.

Some of these tiles are quite strong, while others are so weak that you can break them with your hands. All of them need to be cut using a wet-cutting masonry saw or a grinder equipped with a masonry blade.

Cutting Slate

Whether you rent or buy a wet tile saw, follow instructions carefully. These saws use expensive diamond blades. The most important thing is to keep the blade wet at all times; even a few seconds of dry cutting can dull the blade appreciably. For some models, you will place a pump into a bucket of water next to the saw. With other models, keep a tray under the blade filled with water to the correct level.

Move the tile through the saw blade slowly. Even if the water is running, pushing for a quick cut will lead to dry cutting. If you have a lot of cutting to do, change the water when it gets murky; excessive particles in the water can also dull the blade.

Though it can cut through stone, a wet saw is surprisingly safe to use. You can even touch the blade with your finger while it is running.

A tile saw is the most reliable way to make precise, straight cuts in slate or other stone tile. But you can also use a grinder or a circular saw with a masonry blade. This will create a good deal of dust, so work outside, and wear protective clothing and glasses.

Two sizes of slate tiles present a rough and naturally variegated contrast to a frame made of green glass mosaics bordered by metal rail tiles.

Achieving a Level Surface

If you must install tiles of unequal thickness next to each other, apply the minimum amount of thinset to the wall, and install the thick tiles first. To install the thinner tiles, you can then apply a thicker layer of thinset to the wall, or back-butter the tiles. (See Step 7 on page 105.)

Creating a Finished Edge

If an edge of the backsplash will be exposed, round it over for a finished appearance.

Use another tile to draw a line one tile's thickness away from the edge

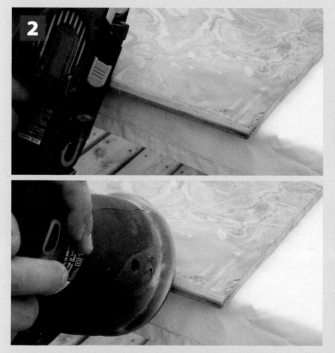

Use a belt sander with 80-grit paper to roughly round the edge, sanding until you meet the line you drew (top). Use a random-orbit sander or a hand sander with 120-grit paper to finish rounding the edge (bottom).

Wet the edge to get an idea of how it will look once sealer is applied. You may need to sand away scratches using 180-grit paper.

Installing Slate

• Slate tiles • Measuring tape • Wet-cutting masonry saw or circular saw with masonry blade • Thinset mortar • Bucket for mixing mortar and grout

1 Take the tiles out of their boxes and arrange them in an appealing line-up that will be fairly easy to install. Mix up the colors so you don't end up, for instance, with two primarily gray or brown tiles right next to each other. You may also plan to install tiles of similar thickness next to each other.

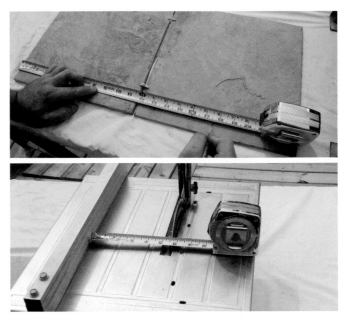

2 Measure from the bottom to the top of the backsplash, and decide on a tile arrangement: here, tiles of two heights, in an alternating pattern. When measuring, position tiles next to each other with the spacers between them (top). Rent a wet-cutting tile saw, or buy an inexpensive model. Measure and position the guard (bottom). Make sure the guard is parallel with the blade, and clamp it firmly in place.

5 Mix a batch of thinset mortar to the consistency of mayonnaise. Using a square-notched trowel, press the mortar against the wall; then tilt the trowel away from the wall, and comb the thinset. In most places, scrape the trowel's teeth gently against the wall. If you want a thicker layer, don't scrape. Work to achieve a smooth, even surface.

6 Start setting tiles in the mortar, using plastic spacers to maintain consistently wide grout lines. To ensure that tiles adhere, back-butter them by applying a thin coat of thinset before pressing them into place. If a tile is thinner than one next to it, back-butter a thick layer of thinset.

• Notched trowel • Plastic tile spacers • 2x4 or 2x6 • Grout and grout float • Large sponge • Stone or masonry sealer and brush

3 Position four or more tiles in a dry run to make sure that the cuts are correct. Using spacers, hold a tile in place to mark for going around obstructions like electrical receptacles or switches. Make sure you leave enough room for reattaching the device's mounting screws.

4 To cut out a notch, first make the two outside cuts, taking care not to cut too far. Then make a series of closely spaced cuts inside the notched area. Break the pieces off with your fingers (inset). To clean up a ragged edge, scrape the edge across the blade, just barely pressing against the blade as you do so.

7 Press or tap the tiles using a flat 2x4 or 2x6 to ensure adhesion and to achieve an even surface (top). If a tile is too low, pry it out; add more mortar to its back; then reinstall. Allow the mortar to harden for a day or so before grouting. Natural stone will soak up grout, creating a "grout haze" that is difficult to clean, so apply a coat or two of masonry sealer (bottom).

8 Mix a batch of latex- or polymer-fortified sanded grout. Follow the procedure in Steps 7, 8, 9, and 10 on pages 100–101. Allow to dry completely; then buff the surface with a dry cloth.

Backsplash with Pattern

Backsplash tile possibilities are pretty much endless. A backsplash does not come in for much abuse, so you can use soft wall tiles, floor tiles, countertop tiles—pretty much anything.

You install ceramic tiles using most of the same techniques as for mosaics or stone tile. Some ceramic tiles have "lugs"—small bumps on their edges—that space them apart to create consistent ⅛-inch-wide grout lines. Others need to be spaced using plastic tile spacers.

The project featured on the following pages shows installing an ensemble that includes field tiles, diamond-shaped insets, decorative tiles, rope detail tiles, and decorative edging. If you instead install just field tiles and perhaps bullnose edging, installation will be simpler.

Notching Tile

To make a cutout or notch in soft wall tile, use a rod saw, which is simply a cylindrical blade attached to a hacksaw. Hold the tile firm and still while you cut.

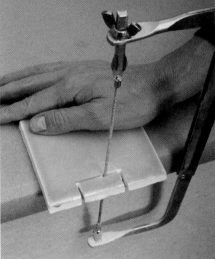

Italianate tile ensembles are easy to find these days. This grouping includes stone-look ceramic tiles with various accents, some of which have botanical features.

Cutting Ceramic Tile with a Snap Cutter

You can straight-cut most ceramic tiles using a snap cutter. Position the tile in the cutter; move the cutting wheel to the bottom of the tile; press down with medium force; and push forward to score a line ❶. Though it may not seem as if you've cut deeply enough, you need do this only once as long as the score line goes all the way across the tile ❷. To make the final separating cut, move the cutting wheel past the tile; position the "wings" over the scored line; and press down on the handle with increasing force until the tile snaps in two. ❸

Installing a Ceramic-Tile Backsplash

- Snap cutter or tile saw • Ceramic tiles • Thinset mortar or organic mastic • Notched trowel • Plastic spacers
- Latex- or polymer-fortified grout • Grout float or squeegee • Sponge and bucket • Grout sealer

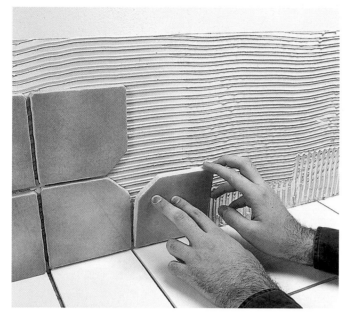

1 After you've laid out the tiles in a dry run and made the necessary cuts in them, apply thinset or mastic to the wall using a notched trowel of the size recommended for your tile. Press the field tiles into the adhesive. If your tiles do not have self-spacing features, use plastic tile spacers at each corner.

2 Pull one or two away from the wall to make sure the adhesive is covering at least 75% of the back of the tile; if not, you may need to back-butter the tiles. Press decorative insets into the openings created by pretrimmed tiles. Take care that these are centered in the openings. You may need to use small shims made of cardboard to hold them in place.

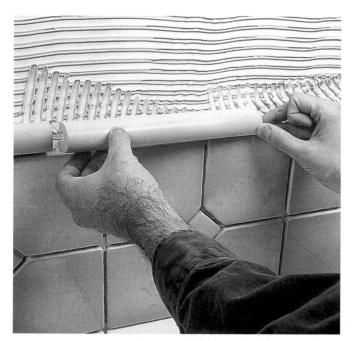

3 Set intermediate trim tiles, like this rope tile, using plastic spacers to maintain consistent grout lines.

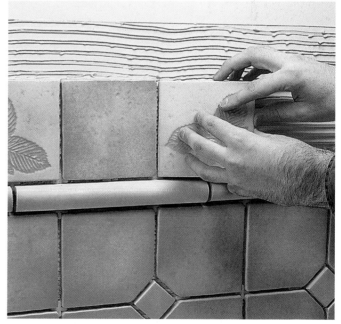

4 Set a row of decorative tiles where desired—in this case, above the row of rope tiles.

Continued on next page

Installing a Ceramic-Tile Backsplash, cont'd.

5 Where tiles do not meet the bottom of wall cabinets, add a row of trim tiles.

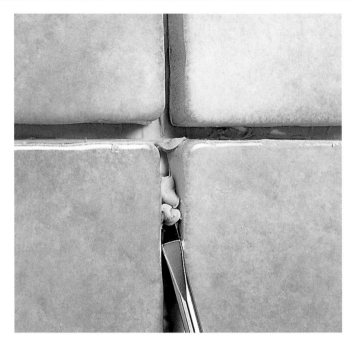

6 All thinset or mastic should be at least ⅛ in. below (or behind) the surface of the tiles, or it may show through the grout. Where it protrudes, use a small screwdriver or knife to scrape it away.

9 Wipe the wall with a clean, damp sponge, which you will need to rinse often. Clean the tile several times to remove most of the surface haze.

10 Squint carefully, and work to achieve grout lines of consistent depth and texture. If the sponge doesn't do the trick, try using a slightly rounded object, such as the handle of a toothbrush.

7 Mix a batch of grout to the consistency of toothpaste or mayonnaise, and load it onto a grout float.

8 Holding the float nearly flat and moving it at an upward angle, push the grout into the joints. Then tilt the float up to scrape away as much excess grout as possible.

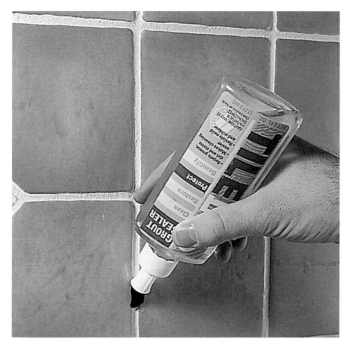

11 Allow the grout to dry; then polish the surface using a soft cloth. Wait a few days; then apply grout sealer.

Finishing Edges

TIP

Where tiles rise up to meet wall cabinets, you can use field tiles (that is, the "normal" tiles). If the top or side edge of the backsplash will not bump into a cabinet, wall molding, shelf, or range hood, however, you must decide how you will finish the edge. (Avoid the temptation to simply apply grout to the edge of a field tile. That may sound like a good idea, but it always looks sloppy.) The simplest way to get a good-looking edge is to install bullnose tile, which looks like a field tile but has one rounded, finished edge. Make sure the tiles you choose have bullnose options. If you'll be installing on an outside wall corner, buy a corner tile, also called a down-angle, which has two finished edges.

Another option is to install trim tiles in a contrasting color or shape. These can give you both a clean exposed edge and some accent color.

As a final option, you could finish the edge with a piece of thin wood molding that is painted to match the wall or the tiles.

5 Countertops

Countertops can be replaced with less disruption to the kitchen than you may expect. Chances are that you will replace the backsplash (either a short 4-incher or a countertop-to-wall-cabinet type) at the same time. Removing a countertop usually takes only a few minutes, and almost all new tops can be installed in a day.

The trickiest part will be the sink. You can reinstall the old sink or upgrade to a new one. If you choose to have a self-rimming sink (one with a rim that rests on top of the countertop), you can install any of the DIY-friendly tops shown in this chapter.

If, however, you want an undermount sink (which rests under the countertop), you may need to hire a professional installer because the exposed edges of the countertop around the sink will need to be perfectly finished. You will probably choose a granite or composite slab for the top.

Choosing Countertops

There are a variety of countertop materials. In some cases, only qualified contractors should install the material. But there are a number that are perfect for do-it-yourself installation. The most common countertop options, which we will cover in this chapter, are:

- **Granite** or other stone slab, which is typically installed by pros only
- **Quartz,** a composite product as solid as granite.
- **Laminate** (a.k.a. Formica) tops, which come in a wide variety of designs
- Colorful and sometimes splashy **ceramic tile,** including Saltillos, perhaps with decorative accents
- **Granite tile,** which nearly achieves the stateliness of a granite slab at a fraction of the cost
- **Slate** or other stone tile, with a rustic charm

Countertop Heights

Most kitchen countertops are around 36 inches above the floor, a comfortable working height for most purposes; and this is the height achieved by placing a standard 1½-inch-thick countertop on top of a standard 34½-inch-tall base cabinet.

For work comfort and flexibility, however, most designers recommend having tops at two or more heights in a kitchen. For example, if you are tall, you may prefer a top that is 37 or 38 inches above the floor. The easiest way to add an inch or two is by raising the base cabinets—unscrew them from the wall; set them on pieces of 2-by or other lumber; check for level; and reattach them. You will need to add base trim to cover the resulting gap at the cabinet's toe space.

If you have room, you can add an eating surface by cantilevering the countertop out past the base cabinets by at least 14 inches. A dining surface can be 36 inches high if you plan to use tall 24-inch chairs or stools. However, if you want the eating surface to be the standard 30-inch height (which allows you to use standard 17-inch chairs), you will need to replace the base cabinets with something shorter. You could order custom cabinetry, but a cheaper alternative is to use 30-inch wall cabinets and rest them on 2×4s to create a toe space at the bottom. The cabinets will not be as deep as standard base cabinets, but that will leave you more room to cantilever out for the table.

A granite-tile top (above) has most of the advantages of a granite slab for a fraction of the price. Here, the edging is made using strips of the same tile, for a slab-like appearance.

Wood countertops can work around a sink, as long as the wood is high quality (like the walnut at right) and kept well sealed.

Quartz and other composite tops may have pronounced speckles, or, as shown on the page opposite, be nearly solid in color.

Mix and Match

Not all countertops in a kitchen need to be made of the same material. In fact, there is a growing trend toward mixing and matching tops. Mixing materials can perk up the design, giving the kitchen a cheerful eclectic appeal.

All of the countertop types shown in this chapter can coexist beautifully with each other as long as you choose colors carefully. In particular, wood countertops go well with just about any other material. Granite slabs or tiles—especially if they have a subtle speckled rather than distinctively veined look—are almost as universally harmonious. For a more playful effect, consider using two different tones of stone slab or tile, or contrasting colors of ceramic tile.

Countertop Coatings

Several companies offer products that can be applied to an old laminate countertop to produce the look of granite or other natural stone. If applied correctly, thoroughly preparing the surface and allowing it to dry completely before using, the result will be a reasonably durable surface, one that can last a decade or even more if it doesn't come in for unusual abuse. You'll find these products at a home center or online. These products often come in kit form, with some of the tools you will need. Some types have a fairly solid color; others, like the one shown here, include color chips for a speckled appearance and slight texture.

The countertop can have some cosmetic blemishes, but do not apply a coating over a top that is coming apart. Use 2-part epoxy putty to fill in any holes, and reattach loose laminate using contact cement.

Once sealed and dry, a coated laminate countertop mimics the look of a solid slab. Removing the sink prior to coating will make for a neater job. Products like this are easy to apply and can last for a decade if not subject to unusual abuse.

Applying Countertop Coating

• Countertop coating kit • Sanding block or random-orbit sander with sandpaper • Paint brush and roller • Painter's tape
• Gloves • Vacuum • Dropcloth

1 Clean the countertop thoroughly. Thoroughly sand the surface using 80-grit sandpaper or the sanding tool supplied in the kit. Use plenty of pressure and work in a circular motion. Cover the entire surface with visible scratches. Vacuum; then use a damp rag to clear away dust. Test with your finger to be sure all dust is removed.

2 Mask the sink, adjacent walls, cabinets below, and any nearby appliances, and place a dropcloth on the floor. Mix the base coat as directed. Use a brush to apply base coat to the backsplash, around the sink, and to any other areas not reachable with a roller. Apply base coat with a roller; then use the brush again to fill in any gaps.

3 Load the color chips into the dispersing tool, or plan to scatter the chips by hand. Spray the base coat with wetting agent; then scatter color ships evenly onto the surface. Completely cover the surface with the chips. Allow 12 to 24 hours for the surface to dry thoroughly.

4 Vacuum away all loose color chips. Scrape the surface to loosen incompletely adhered chips, and vacuum again. Then use the sanding tool or a sanding block to smooth the surface. Apply light to medium pressure and circular motions. The surface should feel slightly textured. Vacuum again; then wipe with a damp cloth.

5 Mix the two parts of the top coat, and apply using a paintbrush and a foam roller. Aim at a uniformly thick coating. Finish by rolling lightly over the entire surface, moving in one direction. Allow to dry overnight; then remove the painter's tape. Wait for a full week before using and wiping the surface.

Painting Laminate Countertops

Serious remodelers may howl with disapproval, but the fact is that laminate countertops can and have been painted, and the results can be more than satisfactory. If you sand the top and apply high-quality primer, the paint will adhere firmly and will peel off only with determined scraping. Paint quality has improved in recent years.

If the painted top comes in for normal wear and tear, it will need to be sanded and repainted every few years. Painting can be a good temporary solution—say, if you plan to replace dreary countertops eventually but don't have the bucks right now. Painting can provide a face-lift that improves your morale and that of your kitchen.

Simply applying a coat of durable paint to a laminate countertop brightens a kitchen in short order.

Cutting Board Insert

TIP

If you're thinking of painting your counter, you might want to consider adding a cutting board insert at the same time. To install, position the manufacturer's template on the countertop and trace around it. Check to make sure that you will not cut through cabinet framing; then use a drill and saber saw to cut the hole. Use silicone sealer to secure the metal tray to the counter; the cutting board can be removed for cleaning.

Repairing a Laminate Top

To reattach laminate that has come loose, or to relaminate delaminated laminate, gently pry it up, and then scrape and brush away any loose debris ❶. Press the laminate back into place, and check that it is smooth. Heat up an iron to the COTTON setting, and press it into the area ❷. Keep the iron moving so it doesn't burn the laminate. Often, this will liquefy the cement so that it will stick again.

If that doesn't work, pry up and apply contact cement to the underside of the laminate and to the substrate ❸. (You can buy contact cement in a small tube.) Allow the cement to dry to the touch; then press the laminate back into place ❹.

Repair a small hole or dent with two-part epoxy auto body or wood filler. Mix the two parts; then apply the filler so that it is slightly raised above the surface. When it starts to harden and is warm, scrape it nearly smooth, leaving it a tiny bit raised. Allow it to dry fully; then sand it smooth.

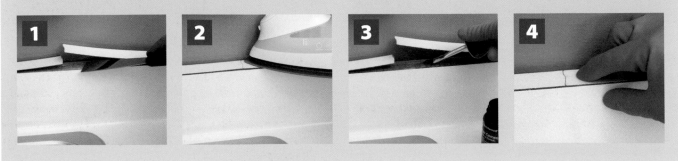

Painting Laminate Countertops

• Sanding block or random-orbit sander with 100-grit sandpaper • Paintbrush and fine-nap roller • TSP or other heavy-duty cleaner • Denatured alcohol • Alcohol-based primer or primer made for plastic surfaces • Paint made for plastic surfaces or acrylic or alkyd paint • Clear polyurethane

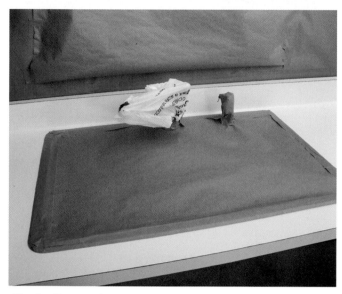

1 Ideally, you should remove the sink and reinstall it after painting. But careful masking is also acceptable. Apply masking tape around a sink, pressing firmly so that paint cannot seep under it. Also apply masking tape against the wall. If caulk at the wall is peeling or damaged, scrape it away and recaulk the area after painting.

2 Clean the top with TSP or degreaser; then rinse it with denatured alcohol, and dry the area thoroughly. Sand the surface with a hand sander or random-orbit sander equipped with 100- or 80-grit sandpaper. When you finish, the whole surface should exhibit scratch marks. Wipe away all dust using a rag dampened with denatured alcohol.

3 Apply a coat of primer that is made to enhance adhesion. Good options include alcohol-based primer (also called white shellac), "plastic paint primer," and oil- or alkyd-based primer. Apply using a small thin-nap roller where possible (the type shown in the next step), or spray it on.

4 Apply a scrubbable paint, such as 100-percent acrylic semigloss or a paint made for cabinets. Allow it to dry thoroughly. Once it is dry to the touch, direct a fan at it and do not touch the paint for 2 days. You may choose to cover the surface with clear polyurethane for extra protection. For the next week, avoid placing heavy objects on it, and wipe it only very gently.

Substrates for Tile Countertops

The three projects that follow this one—ceramic tile, granite tile, and slate tile—are installed on top of the substrate shown in these pages. Countertop tiles must rest on a subsurface that is very strong; any slight movement can crack grout lines or even tiles. The surface also needs to be even and level, and it should provide backing for the front edge treatment you choose.

Fortunately, building such a substrate is a straightforward project, calling for one layer of ¾-inch plywood topped by a layer of ½-inch cement-fiber backer board. In most cases, the countertop will be 25 inches deep, so it overhangs the base cabinets by an inch or so.

Removing the Old Countertop. Start by removing the existing top. If there is a sink, disconnect the trap; turn off the hot and cold water supplies; and disconnect the supply tubes. Next, disconnect the dishwasher drain tube and the electrical connection to the waste-disposal unit, if your kitchen has these. You may choose to leave the sink attached to the top, or remove it; you will probably need to unscrew mounting clips that hold the sink to the top; then pry the sink away.

Hold a level on top of the base cabinets to be sure they are level in both directions. Also ensure that they are firmly attached and do not wobble. If you need to make adjustments, remove the screws that attach them to the wall; use shims to make them level; and reattach by driving screws into wall studs.

This granite-tile top looks great because the subsurface is perfectly level and even.

Start Out Square and Straight

If a wall is wavy or if a corner is not straight, then the finished tile surface will reflect these imperfections; you may end up with noticeably curved lines or oddly shaped tiles at the back of the countertop. If the wall problems are only minor or the tiles are relatively large, the imperfections will be less visible. The only way to tell for sure is to lay out the tiles on the plywood in a dry run (before you attach the plywood), along with the backsplash material. Stand back, and take a look. If you don't like what you see, take steps to straighten out the wall, either by applying joint compound or (in extreme cases) by removing drywall and installing shims on the studs to straighten things out.

Supporting the Cut

When you cut a hole for the sink opening, the cutout section will start to sag as you near the end of the cut. The blade may bind, and the cut piece may tear as it starts to fall. To avoid this, use a temporary cleat: When you start to cut the last side of the opening, place a scrap piece, a few inches longer than the cutout, over the opening as shown. Drive two screws to attach the cutout piece to the scrap piece. Now it will stay put as you finish the cut.

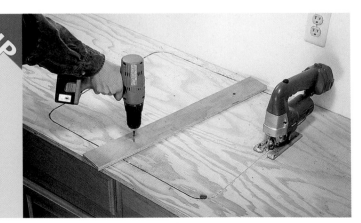

Building a Substrate for a Tile Countertop

• Level • ¾-inch plywood • Table or circular saw • Glue and construction adhesive • Drill-driver and screws • The sink you will install
• Carpenter's square • Saber saw • Plastic sheeting or roofing felt • Utility knife • Staple gun • Thinset mortar
• Square-notched trowel • ½-inch backer board • Fiberglass mesh tape

1 Using a table saw or circular saw, cut pieces of plywood (not particleboard or oriented-strand board) to fit. Make sure all of the pieces are supported within 3 in. of their ends by a cabinet. Also rip strips of plywood about 3 in. wide to use for reinforcing.

2 Reinforce the plywood by attaching the strips to the underside of the plywood. First attach strips around the perimeter; then install crosspieces that will fall over the cabinet frames. Apply wood glue; then drive 1 ¼-inch screws.

3 Test to make sure that the pieces will fit, with crosspieces resting on top of cabinet frames. Remove the plywood, and apply construction adhesive on the cabinet frames.

4 Drive screws up through corner braces inside the cabinets. Use screws that drive most—but not all—the way through the doubled plywood. Also drive screws down through the top of the plywood into solid wood cabinet supports (but not into particleboard frames).

Continued on next page

Building a Substrate for a Tile Countertop, cont'd.

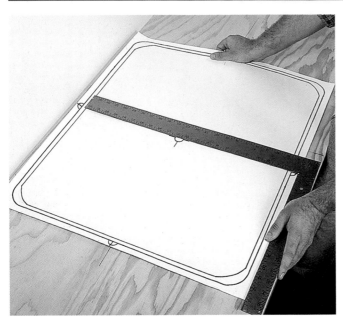

5 Set the sink you will install upside down on a piece of cardboard, and trace its outline. Then draw a line an inch or so inside that line to mark the actual cut line. Mark the centers of the front and back. Place the cardboard on the plywood, and determine its position (above a sink base, which has no drawers).

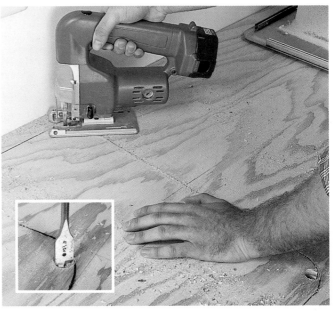

6 Mark the cutout line; then place the sink upside down on it to be sure it will fit, with the sink's lip resting on the counter. Drill one or more starter holes, large enough for your saber-saw blade, on the inside of the cut line (inset). Cut the hole using a saber-saw. Work slowly at the corners while you rotate the saw. As you near the end of the cut, support the cutout so it doesn't fall heavily and possibly crack the plywood. (See "Support the Cut," page 118.)

9 Working with a helper, set the backer-board pieces in the mortar. Set them straight down, and avoid sliding them more than an inch or so. Leave a $1/16$-in. gap between the pieces.

10 Around the sink cutout, add narrow strips to the front and back. Drive backer-board screws in a 12-in. grid to attach the backer board to the plywood.

7 Staple a moisture-resistant membrane over the plywood. Use 14-lb. roofing felt (tar paper) or 4-mil polyethylene sheeting.

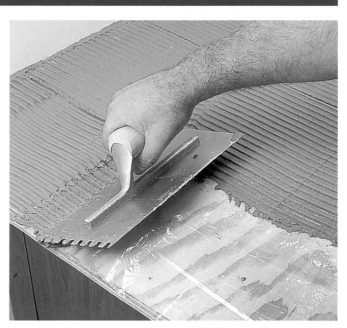

8 Cut pieces of cement-fiber backer board to fit, with joints offset at least 2 in. from the joints in the plywood. Test to be sure that the pieces will fit; then set them aside. Use a square-notched trowel to spread, then comb, an even layer of thinset mortar over the membrane.

11 Fill the 1/16-in. gaps between the backer-board pieces with thinset mortar, using the flat side of the trowel. Cut and lay pieces of fiberglass mesh tape over the seams.

12 Also cover the edge pieces with fiberglass mesh. Press the mesh in place; then spread a thin layer of thinset over it.

Ceramic-Tile Countertop

Tile countertops are more popular in some parts of the country than others, but they are a practical and attractive choice anywhere. The tiles themselves—especially if they are glazed—are durable and easy to keep clean. And if you fill the joints with epoxy or latex-reinforced grout and apply sealer a couple times a year, the entire surface will effectively resist stains and be easy to keep clean.

Choose tiles that are made for use on countertops or floors. Do not use soft wall tiles; they will almost certainly crack eventually. With so many ceramic color options, you can create a top that is muted and neutral or one that is a riot of splashy color or something in between.

Start with a firm substrate. Check that it has square corners and that the back wall is parallel with the front edge; otherwise, you can wind up with unattractively crooked lines.

Avoid Surprises

Lay out the job as completely as possible before you start spreading the thinset. To be safe, you may choose to set all or most of the tiles on the countertop in a dry run, with the plastic spacers. Then pick up one section of tiles; spread mortar; reset the tiles; and continue in this way for the entire top.

A countertop and back wall, left, is tiled in pastel hues. The front edge is finished with special nosing pieces, and an apron of mosaic tiles extends downward the same width as the apron sink.

Above, cheery blue-and-white tiles have a glossy finish that is easy to keep clean. The edges are finished with V-cap tiles, which have a raised edge that keeps spills from running onto the floor.

Applying and Maintaining Grout

Mix and apply latex- or epoxy-fortified grout, and apply it using a grout float. Press into place; then scrape away most of the excess. Use a damp sponge, continually rinsed, to wipe the surface and produce grout lines that are consistent in depth.

After a week or so, apply grout sealer to the surface to make the grout stain resistant. Reapply grout sealer every 6 months to a year or so.

Important Layout Details

When marking layout lines, take into account the thickness of the grout lines. Also keep in mind that the thickness of the mortar will bring the front edge pieces outward about 1/8 inch.

Edges and Backsplashes

At a home center or tile store you can choose an ensemble of tiles that match or complement each other. You'll need field tiles (regular tiles with four unfinished edges) as well as special tiles to create finished front and side edges. (See below.) V-cap edging is the easiest to install (though you will need a wet-cutting tile saw to cut it) and provides a raised rim to keep small spills from running over the edge. Other options include a combination of bullnose tile and trim tile, or wood edging.

Also plan for the backsplash. (See below.) If you choose to install a countertop-to-cabinet backsplash, see Chapter 3 for instructions; you can wait until later to install it. With ceramic tile, however, it often looks neatest when you install a short backsplash using tiles of the same or complementary colors. In that case, they should be installed at the same time as the countertop. A capped top lends a substantial feel. You'll need to install a strip of backer board to support it. Coved base is the easiest to wipe clean

because it forms a curve rather than 90-degree corner at the bottom. However, it is the most difficult to install because the field tiles that abut it must be cut perfectly. Bullnose tile is the easiest to install.

Front Edge Options

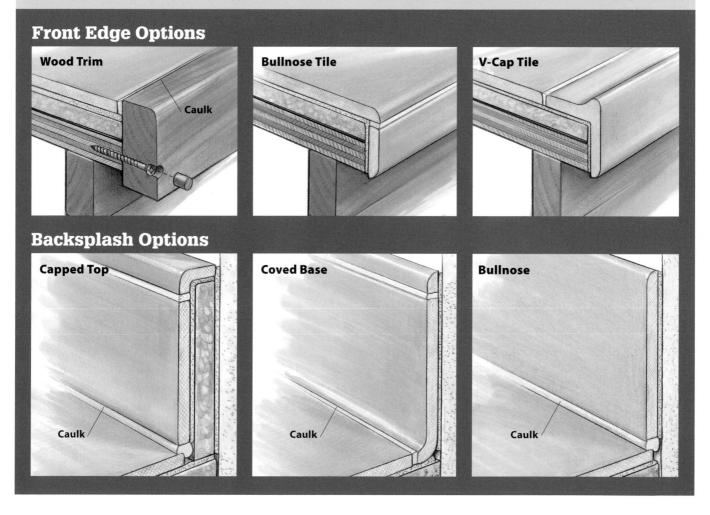

Wood Trim — Caulk

Bullnose Tile

V-Cap Tile

Backsplash Options

Capped Top — Caulk

Coved Base — Caulk

Bullnose — Caulk

Installing Ceramic Tile

• Field tiles • Edge tiles and backsplash tiles • Chalk-line box and pencil • Framing square • Thinset mortar

1 Use an edging piece to establish a working line for the main field of full tiles. Slide the edging piece along with a pencil to make the mark.

2 Snap chalk guidelines to continue the edge lines. Use a carpenter's square to check for square, or set a number of tiles in a dry run.

3 Mix a batch of thinset mortar to the consistency of toothpaste. Starting at a point that controls the layout—usually, an inside corner—use a notched trowel to spread the mortar, then comb it with the trowel's teeth grazing the backerboard.

7 Cut the tile one grout line's width shorter than the mark. Most tiles can be straight-cut using a snap cutter.

8 For applying mortar in narrow spaces, a detail trowel is easier to use. If any thinset starts to harden; scrape it off; mix a new batch; and apply fresh thinset.

9 Press the cut tiles in place, and use a straightedge or flat board to make sure that they are on the same plane as the full tiles.

• Notched trowel and small detail trowel • Plastic spacers • Short 2x4 tapping board • Snap tile cutter • Wet tile saw

4 Embed the first rows of field tiles along the guidelines. Periodically use a framing square to check the alignment of the grout seams and to ensure straight lines.

5 Continue working to set all of the full-size field tiles. Tap with a flat board to make sure the surface is even, and use a straightedge to maintain straight lines.

6 To mark for cutting a tile, set a full tile on top of the next-to-last one so that it butts against the wall. Mark where the two tiles meet.

10 Butter the backs of V-cap or other edging with thinset. If the grout line ends up too narrow, add even more thinset.

11 Take special care to make sure that the edge tiles are completely embedded in wet thinset. Examine the joints closely to make sure they are perfect; they will be on display for years.

12 At an inside corner, cut two pieces at a 45-deg. angle. This is a tricky spot and will be highly visible, so take the time to work carefully, and recut new pieces if your first attempts are not perfect.

Granite Tile

Granite tile, carefully installed, creates a sumptuous countertop surface for a fraction of the cost of a granite slab. Home centers and tile stores carry a wide array of colors and patterns. Most come in batches that contain tiles that are remarkably consistent in appearance. Because granite tends to be speckled rather than veined, side-by-side tiles look remarkably like a continuous surface.

Granite is strong, dense, and moisture resistant, making it a practical countertop tile material. Quartzite is also a good practical choice, but because of its veined pattern, it will create a checkerboard-like tiled pattern rather than a continuous surface.

Granite tile can be installed much like ceramic tile. Set the tile in a bed of thinset mortar using spacers to maintain ⅛-inch joints, and fill the joints with grout. The following pages show a different technique, however: setting granite tiles in silicone sealer rather than mortar and butting the pieces tight against each other. The resulting surface will have no grout lines, though the chamfered edges of the tiles will make the joints somewhat apparent.

This unusual arrangement combines brown ceramic V-cap tiles with granite field tiles.

Edging Options

In the following steps, the front edge is finished with a narrow piece of tile tucked under overhanging tiles to create the illusion of a solid granite surface. Another option is to run the tiles up to the edge of the subsurface, then attach a wood strip about 1/16 inch below the tile surface ❶; a biscuit joiner will enable you to attach it without visible fastener heads. Or you can sometimes buy V-cap molding made of the same granite as the tiles ❷; install it as you would a tiled countertop (pages 122-25). A third option is to buy metal edging, which is attached to the substrate prior to installing the tiles ❸.

Installing Granite Tile

- Level and straightedge • Plywood, backer board, and screws for making the subsurface • Wet-cutting tile saw • Granite tile
- Power sander and hand sander with various grits of sandpaper • Vacuum, rag, and mineral spirits • Painter's tape
- Caulk gun with 100-percent silicone caulk • Flat board for bedding tiles • Lacquer, sealer, brushes

1 Following the steps shown on pages 118–121, remove the old countertop and replace it with a substrate made of ¾-in. plywood and ½-in. cement-fiber backer board. For this project it is especially important that the subsurface be level and flat in both directions. If it is not, shim the cabinets.

2 Measure and cut tiles using a wet-cutting tile saw. The overall width of a countertop is typically 25 to 26 in. (depending on the type of edging you choose), so there will probably be a row of narrow tiles against the wall.

3 If some tile edges will be exposed, sand the edges with a belt or random-orbit sander to achieve a smooth surface. Start with 100-grit paper; then move on to 180, 220, and 320 grits. The result will not be as shiny as the tile surface, but it will be less dull, and you can achieve a final luster with a coat of clear lacquer (Step 10).

4 Vacuum away all dust, and wipe with a rag dampened with paint thinner or mineral spirits. It is important that the surface be completely free of dust to ensure that the silicone adheres firmly

Continued on next page

Installing Granite Tile, cont'd.

5 Cut and lay all of the tiles in a dry run on the counter. If there's an inside corner, it's best to start there. Use pieces of tape to hold the lower edging pieces in place. (The thickness of the silicone will bring these pieces out about $\frac{1}{8}$ in., so have the top tiles overhang them by that much during layout.) If you will install wood edging, press it in place to check for correct alignment.

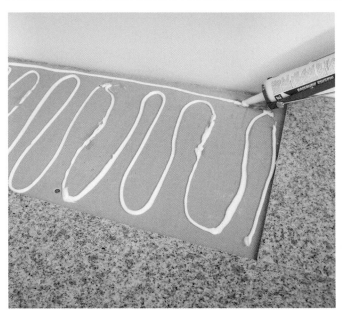

6 Double-check that the dry-laid tiles are in perfect alignment. Remove two to four tiles, keeping the others in place. With a caulk gun, apply squiggles of clear silicone caulk (it looks white at first) spaced no more than $1\frac{1}{2}$ in. apart in the area. Aim to keep the thickness of the caulk consistent.

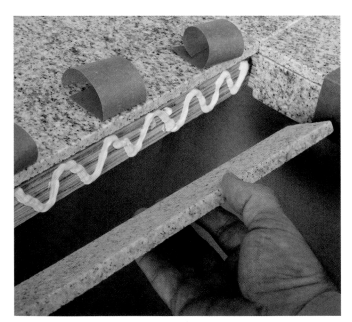

9 Apply a pattern of evenly spaced squiggles to the edge of the substrate, and press the edging pieces into it, up under the front tiles. Use pieces of tape to hold them in place. The top tiles should just barely overhang the edge pieces—by $\frac{1}{32}$ in. or so. Check this alignment carefully; you may need to remove tape, adjust, and reapply tape several times.

10 If there are exposed edges, use an artist's paintbrush to apply two or three coats of clear lacquer to them. This will make them shine like the rest of the tiles.

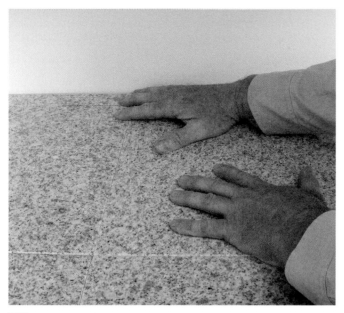

7 Lower the tiles back onto the silicone, and press to seat them. They should be butted tightly against each other and against the unglued tiles. If one tile is significantly lower than others, pry it up and apply more silicone as needed.

8 Install four or so more tiles in the same way. Press—and if needed, tap—a straight board at several points and in several directions to achieve a smooth overall surface. You have about one-half hour to work and make adjustments before the silicone starts to harden.

11 Allow a couple of days for the silicone to set firmly. Apply stone sealer to the surface. Apply several coats to the joints, to completely fill them. Reapply sealer every 6 months or so.

Dealing with Irregular Tiles **TIP**

Granite tiles are usually wonderfully flat and square. However, some types may vary slightly in thickness. If some tiles are thinner than others, it is usually best to place them in the back of the installation; and remember, you will need to apply the silicone a little thicker for them.

More Countertop-Tile Options

Most tiled tops are made of ceramic or granite, but there are other options worth considering as well. These two pages show a smattering of available options; a trip to a tile center will yield a wider array of choices.

Because kitchen countertops typically occupy a fairly small amount of square footage, you may be able to fit some pretty pricy tiles into your budget. (A professionally installed granite slab will usually run at least $35 per square foot, while even high-end granite tiles will usually run less than $8.)

Most people prefer a countertop that is as smooth as possible. But tiles with a pronounced texture can be nearly as easy to wipe clean, as long as the texture does not include holes and valleys where crumbs can collect. Some natural tiles need to be sealed every few months, which may sound like a chore. But sealing usually takes little more time than regular cleaning—however, you will need to put up a sign telling people not to use the counter for a few hours while the sealer dries.

Slate

Slate tiles vary greatly in color, texture, and regularity. Tiles that are irregular in size and thickness with deep texture are suitable for a backsplash (see pages 102–105) but not for a countertop. And some slate tiles are so weak you could break them with your hands. But many slate tiles are strong and have a texture that is more wavy than creviced, so they can give you a nice rustic appearance while being fairly easy to wipe clean. And slate can be very inexpensive.

Tumbled Tiles

Tumbled tiles (sometimes called by other terms, like honed or sand-blasted) have a rough-looking surface that is gentle to the touch. They are made of travertine, marble, granite, limestone, or other natural stone. Tumbled tiles should be kept well protected with regular applications of stone sealer. You can also buy ceramic or porcelain tiles with the same look; they do not require sealing.

Mosaic Tile

A mosaic-tile countertop has small tiles and plenty of grout lines, which scares many people off. But if you apply the grout carefully and apply sealer a few times a year, the surface will be fairly easy to keep clean. And a mosaic surface creates plenty of visual interest. Some sheets have tiles as large as 4 inches square, while others may be smaller. The tiles themselves may be glazed ceramic, natural stone, porcelain, or other materials.

Mosaic tiles most often come in 12 x 12-inch sheets, and so are easier to install than you may think. Install a backer-board substrate, and lay out as you would for standard tiles. See pages 98-101 for installation tips. To make the tiles fit, you may be able to get away with simply cutting the mesh backing, or you may need to cut individual tiles. It's important to apply thinset mortar that is just thick and wet enough so all of the tiles adhere securely—but not so thick and wet that mortar oozes up through the many grout lines.

Edging for a mosaic-tile surface calls for special attention. In most cases you cannot use V-cap or bullnose tiles to easily create a smooth edge. You may choose to use more of the mosaic tiles for the edge, in which case you will end up with unfinished tile edges and a line of grout along the corner. This has a casual look, but if you apply the grout carefully, it is just as cleanable as a more finished-looking edge. Or buy bullnose pieces of

the same color (if they are available) and perhaps add a strip of different-colored tiles below the bullnoses. Another common option is to use a strip of wood or metal edging, as seen below.

Pebble mosaics (above) come in odd-shaped strips that interlock rather than rectangular strips. You'll need to cut these using a wet saw. Because they are rough, exposed edges can be sanded to look just fine.

Granite and Other Stone Slab Countertops

Granite slab countertops are, in many people's minds, the pinnacle of taste and luxury, and along with the natural beauty comes great practicality. A good granite top should be sealed once in a while, but then is very easy to clean; and it's extremely strong, to boot.

Some people think that the less expensive granites—especially those from China—are full of voids and weaker than more expensive types. However, the truth is nearly the opposite: Cheaper granite is usually very strong, while exotic and pricy granites sometimes are more fragile (but certainly not always).

You may wonder what they are doing in a book on inexpensive upgrades. This material is indeed at the upper financial limit for this book, but it may not be as expensive as you expect.

On the following four pages we show how pros cut and install granite, and also offer some do-it-yourself options. Here are a few slab options in addition to granite:

■ **Engineered stone,** often referred to as **quartz,** is a man-made product made of quartz or other stone chips captured in a strong resin. This material is growing in popularity for a number of reasons. It has the hardness of granite but with a much more regular pattern that is usually speckled. A supplier can show a wide range of colors, so you can match practically any decor. Because it is manufactured, unlike granite and other natural materials, you can be sure that the slab you get will look very much like the sample you choose. Engineered tops do not have to be sealed like natural stone does.

■ Countertops made from **recycled glass and other materials** are an eco-friendly choice. They often come in splashy colors and have a charming playful quality.

■ **Marble, onyx,** and other stones are often used for countertops in the bathroom or other areas, but usually are not suitable for a kitchen, because they scratch and stain easily.

■ **Soapstone** is a soft stone, but it is even less porous than granite, making it very resistant to staining and burning. The inevitable scratches can be buffed out easily. Some types will deepen in color over time.

Is Granite Green?

In many ways, granite is a very eco-friendly choice. It is one of the most abundant minerals on earth and is found virtually everywhere. Cutting and polishing it creates very little pollution and uses no chemicals.

An engineered-stone slab (left) has a regular speckled pattern. You can choose a plain edging or, as here, a detailed edge.

Natural granite (above) typically has swirls and speckles, often in surprisingly stunning patterns.

Slab Strategies

Here are some ways to get granite into your kitchen:

■ Hire a company to do it all. The installers will make a template of walls and install a top—and usually, a 4- to 5-inch tall backsplash—with holes for a sink. If you have an under-mounted sink, they will attach it as well but will probably not hook up the plumbing. Some companies will install for as little as $30 per square foot but will no doubt charge more if you want an under-mounted sink (which requires buffing the exposed countertop edge).

■ Order slabs cut to fit from a company, and install them yourself. Some online sources will ask for a cardboard template to avoid mis-fit problems. Arrange for delivery to your house, if possible. Have several strong-backed helpers on hand to hoist the slabs into place, and work carefully; you can easily break a slab, especially near a sink hole.

■ Buy a preformed slab and do some cutting yourself. Some stone stores sell these. Or order a preformed slab from an online source. You can choose whether to have only the front edge finished, or pay a bit more to have one or both of the sides finished. Slabs are typically 8 feet long. A side that abuts a wall or an appliance does not have to be finished; you can cut it yourself following the instructions shown below. As the following pages show, it is feasible for a capable and careful do-it-yourselfer to cut a hole for a self-rimming (drop-in) sink, but polishing the edges for an under-mounted sink is a job best left to pros.

Cutting Slabs to Size

Cutting slabs to width and finishing the front edge is a job for professional fabricators, who often use an industrial-size wet saw (below left).

You can make straight cuts on a quartz or granite slab yourself. Buy a diamond blade (for about $35), and install it in a good-quality circular saw. Draw the cut line using a pencil or yellow crayon. Clamp a straightedge guide to help you stay on the line. Have a helper direct a weak spray of water at the blade while you cut. Avoid over-spraying, which can harm the saw's motor, but keep the blade constantly wet. If the waste side is longer than a few inches, support it to avoid cracking the slab when it falls away. Once the slab it cut, smooth the edge using a belt sander, then a random-orbit sander or a hand sander. Start with 80-grit paper, and proceed to 120-, 150-, and 180-grit papers. If the edge will be visible, continue increasing the grits until the surface shines to your satisfaction.

Cutting Out for a Sink

Cutting using a grinder with a diamond blade is not beyond the skills of an experienced handyman; the challenge is to avoid slipping. Hold the grinder firmly at all times because if it slips forward even once you can ruin the slab. Practice on scrap pieces until you feel confident of your skills.

If your sink does not come with a cardboard template, make one. In the example shown ❶, the countertop will overhang an under-mounted sink; the other option is to have part of the under-mounted sink's top flange visible. If you will install a self-rimming sink, see page 120 for instructions on marking the opening.

Cut about 1/8 in. inside the lines, holding the grinder in a straight vertical position ❷. Dust and granite chips will fly, so wear a dust mask, eye protection, and long-sleeve shirt with heavy clothing. Work carefully to avoid going past the cut line at any point.

At the corner, take your time and don't try to get it all cut on the first pass. Make a series of angled cuts that go just up to within 1/8 inch of the cut lines. Once all four corners have been cut this way, remove the inside waste piece ❸.

Scrape with the grinder to basically clean up the corner to within 1/8 inch of the cut line. Pull rather than push the blade to slowly remove waste ❹.

With the grinder blade held vertically, scrape—again, pulling rather than pushing—to gradually remove the last 1/8 in. of material and reach the cut line ❺. Periodically position the sink to check the fit. If you will install a self-rimming sink, your job is now done.

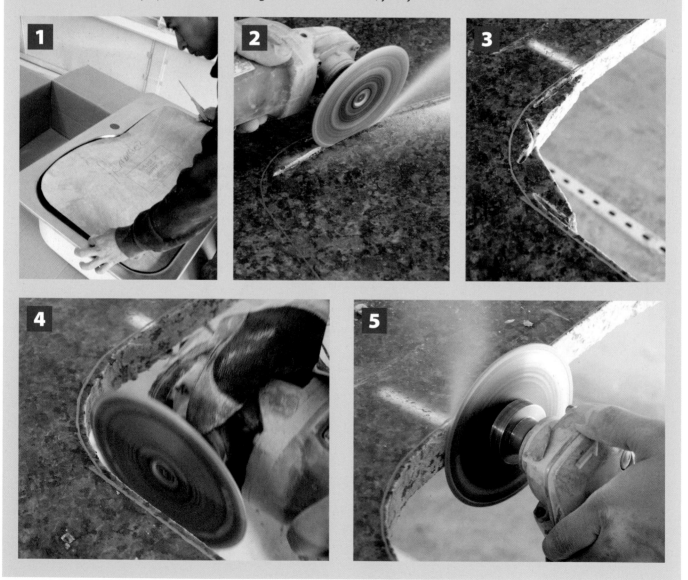

Buffing for an Under-mounted Sink

If you will install an under-mounted sink, the edges of the countertop cutout will be exposed and so must be polished to the same finish as the top of the slab. A very motivated homeowner can accomplish this task, but buying the tools may cost more than hiring someone.

All along the cutout, check that the cut edge is square. Scrape with the grinder as needed to make corrections ❶.

Position the sink to make sure that the cut follows the line. Mark with a crayon any places that need to be cut a bit more, and scrape with the grinder to reach the lines ❷.

Equip the grinder with an abrasive wheel, and use it to start smoothing the edges. Press with only medium pressure, and work slowly, constantly keeping it moving; if you hold it in one place for a few seconds, it may create a wave. Also use the wheel to slightly chamfer the top edge of the hole ❸.

Polish the edges using a wet grinder made for granite polishing. You will need four or five polishing wheels with increasingly fine grits—200, 400, 800, 1,500, and if the 1,500 doesn't make it smooth enough, a 3,000-grit wheel ❹.

Hook the grinder up to water; and start with the 200-grit wheel. Move slowly, and feel with your hands; grind until all along the length the surface feels the same ❺. Then do the same with the 400-, 800-, and 1,500-grit wheels. Make sure you have completely polished with one wheel before moving on to the next one.

Wipe the area dry, and check the sheen. You may or may not need to polish with the 3,000-grit wheel. Rub with 000 steel wool for a final buffing ❻.

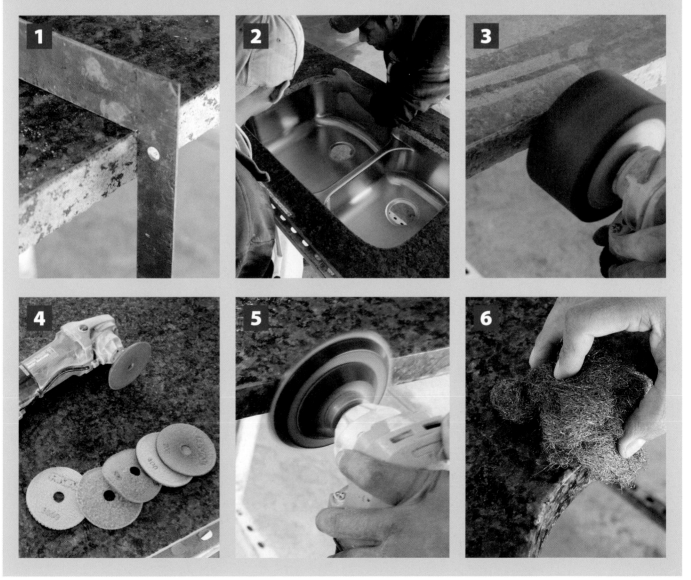

Post-Formed Countertops

Post-formed countertops are covered with a plastic laminate (sometimes referred to as Formica, which is actually a brand name), and have rolled, rather than square, front edges and backsplashes for easy cleaning. Though considered a low-end product, laminate is available in many attractive patterns and colors and will endure decades of normal kitchen wear and tear. It resists most but not all stains and fairly hot pots as well; but if you (or perhaps a teenager in your home) transfer a pot directly from a burner to the countertop, a burn mark may result.

You can buy post-form countertops at a home center. If you need to turn a corner, buy two pieces with mitered corners. To cut a post-form to length, lay it upside-down on a pair of sawhorses, and support the waste side so it will not fall away. Cut using a circular saw, with a clamped straightedge as a guide.

Post-formed laminate countertops have molded front edges and backsplashes. Traditional post-forms have rounded front edges, but many newer types, like this one, have angular chamfered edges for a look that is both more modern and more stone-like.

Installing a Post-Formed Countertop

• Level, pencil, and shims • Post-formed countertop with end strips • Drill-driver with screws • Belt sander
• Caulk gun with adhesive caulk • Household iron

1 Remove the old countertop, and check the cabinets to make sure they are level in both directions. If they are not, install shims at the bottom of the cabinets to make the cabinets level, or place shims on top of the cabinet to level the countertop.

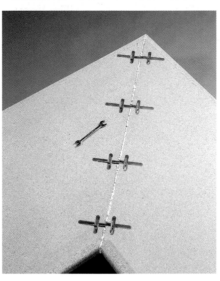

2 To join two mitered pieces to form a corner, set the two pieces upside down on four sawhorses. Apply adhesive caulk to the edges. While a helper crouches below and checks that the two pieces are level with each other, insert I-bolts into the T-slots and tighten with a wrench.

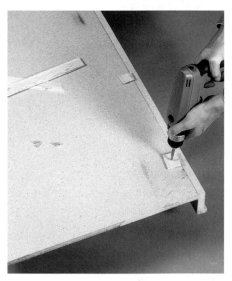

3 If the base cabinets are not 34 in. high or if you need to install shims to level the countertop, cut and attach small shim pieces as needed.

4 Get a couple of helpers to lift and lower the countertop it onto the cabinets. Be sure one person supports any joint. Push the top against the wall. If there are gaps, use a pencil to scribe the top of the backsplash to mimic the wall's contours (inset). Remove the top, and belt-sand it to conform to the scribed line.

5 Replace the countertop. Because the top is heavy, you need only a few screws to hold it in place. Drive them up through the cabinet corner blocks and into the underside of the top. Be sure the screws are not so long that they poke through the surface of the top.

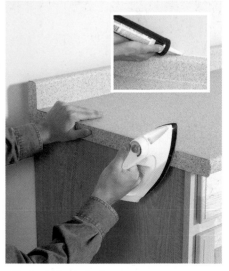

6 Seal the joint between countertop and wall with silicone caulk. Apply a thin bead (inset), then use a damp rag to wipe away the excess and create a neat line. On exposed countertop ends, install preformed end strips that match the top laminate. Use a hot iron to activate the adhesive.

Custom Laminate Countertops

While you may have a limited number of color and pattern options when choosing a post-form laminate countertop, the possibilities are nearly endless if you are willing to make your own top. At a home center or online you can search through hundreds of styles and choose one that is a perfect complement for your kitchen decor.

A custom-made laminate top has square rather than rounded edges at the front and back. You can make a 4-inch-tall backsplash of the same laminate material, or just install a flat top and add a backsplash of another material.

Making your own laminate top calls for good tools and solid basic carpentry skills, but is not difficult. Particleboard is the most common substrate, but you can also use plywood as long as it's very straight and has crisp, 90-degree edges. A router with a roller-guided laminate bit is highly recommended; sanding the edges is possible but will almost certainly lead to less-than-crisp corners. Also, use professional-quality contact cement.

To make the substrate, use two thicknesses of ¾-inch particleboard, or glue 4-inch-wide strips to the bottom of the edges of a single sheet to make 1½-inch-thick ends and sides. Attach the strips using construction adhesive and screws; drill pilot holes before driving the screws to avoid mushrooming the material.

Be Safe

Use contact cement only in well-ventilated areas. Exposure to its fumes can irritate your nose, lungs, and throat. Be sure to wear eye protection and rubber gloves as well.

Custom tops have squared-off edges and typically do not incorporate the backsplash. You can make a separate backsplash using a strip of particleboard and laminate, or as shown here, use a different material for the backsplash.

Making a Laminate Countertop

• ¾-inch particleboard or plywood • 1¼-inch screws and construction adhesive • Power saw for cutting substrate • Utility knife and straightedge • Drill • Laminate • Contact cement and foam brush • Laminate roller • Contact cement • Lattice strips • Router with roller-guided flush-trimming and bevel bits

1 Cut strips of laminate for the countertop edges. Make the strips ¼ in. or so wider than the edge; you can trim the excess later. Hold a straightedge firmly, and score several times using a sharp knife blade. Then snap the sheet along the score line. You can also cut using a table saw.

2 Glue laminate to the substrate using contact cement. Spread the adhesive on both mating surfaces, and allow it to dry until tacky, not sticky.

3 Once pressed into place, the pieces cannot be slid at all. Carefully align the piece; then press gently. Use a laminate roller to roll it smooth. Trim the edges using a router and a flush-trimming bit.

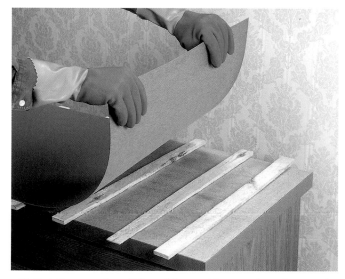

4 Cut the top piece ½ in. wider and longer than the area it will cover. Use a paint roller to apply contact cement to both the substrate and the back of the laminate, and allow it to dry until barely tacky. Place lattice strips on the substrate, and lower the laminate onto them. Make sure the sheet overhangs on all sides. Pull out the strips one at a time. Once the strips are out and you are sure that the top is correctly aligned, press on it; then roll it using a laminate roller.

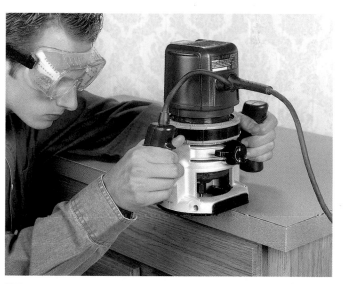

5 Equip a router with a roller-guided bevel bit. Test on scrap pieces, and adjust the height of the bit so that it trims the edges without digging in too deep. Use it to cut off the overhangings at the top and bottom of the edges.

Wood Countertops

Wood slabs composed of narrow pieces laminated together are sometimes called butcher block. They make for stunning countertops, and an 8-foot-long top can be found for under $100. Cutting and installing butcher-block tops is about as easy as it gets.

Are Wood Countertops Durable?

The answer to this question is a bit complicated, but the rewards of buying an inexpensive but great-looking countertop are great enough to warrant some research. The short answer is: If you buy a quality top and treat it right, it should serve you well for many years. The long answer involves several considerations:

- It's usually not a good idea to treat a wood countertop as a cutting board. Doing so will not only make a series of crisscrossed knife lines but allow moisture to penetrate into the wood, which could cause it to warp and even delaminate. Cutting boards are small and often have crisscrossed pieces to keep them from bending and coming apart; a large countertop has no such safeguards.

- Pay attention to the orientation of the wood grain. A quality top will have the individual boards positioned on end—with the narrow side visible on top and the wider side visible only at the end. Flat-laid tops are more likely to warp.

- Buy wood tops from a supplier that specializes in them. Maple butcher block from a lumberyard or supplier of hardwood may sound like a good idea, but these slabs are notorious for coming apart when used as countertops.

- Don't buy a wood top unless you plan to take care of it. Care is usually a simple matter of applying mineral oil or a sealer made for wood tops every couple of months. This is very easy to do—but it's also very easy to forget, and neglect can lead to irreversible damage.

- Wood tops are most practical for portions of the kitchen that won't often get wet. Don't use a wood top around a sink unless you're really good about wiping up water quickly and sealing the top at least once a month. Fortunately, wood goes with just about any other material, so it's almost always a good decorating decision to pair a wood top with a surface made of a different material.

- If a wood top starts to warp or comes apart after a few years, it's not the end of the world. You haven't paid all that much for it, and can easily replace it with a new wood top or a top made from something else.

Wood countertops can have fairly sharp edges, like the one shown at left, or you can use a router or power sander to round off the top edge and corners.

People have long been afraid to use wood countertops near sinks and cooktops, but today's more-durable butcher-block materials inspire a fearless approach, as seen on the page opposite.

Installing a Wood Countertop

• Circular saw, straightedge, and clamps • Level and shims • Wood countertop • Caulk gun with clear silicone sealer or construction

1 Before cutting a wood top, test-cut a scrap piece of wood to see whether your blade creates chips or tear-outs; if so, replace the blade. You want to cut through the thickness of the wood at exactly 90 deg., to create tight miter joints, so check the blade with a square and make any needed adjustments (inset). Set the blade depth so it cuts no more than ¼ in. deeper than the wood thickness; this minimizes tear-out.

2 Check the cabinets for level in both directions, and shim as needed. Either loosen screws holding the cabinets in place and shim the cabinets at the bottom, or install shims that will support the countertop so it is level. Make sure that the countertop will be supported at least every 24 inches; at a corner you may need to attach cleats to the wall.

5 Press the pieces together, and check the alignment. Usually the weight of the pieces will be enough to keep them in place, but you may need to add weights to a smaller piece. Use a solvent-dampened rag to wipe away any excess adhesive.

6 Wait a day or more for the adhesive to completely harden. Sand the surface using a hand sander or random-orbit sander, starting with 80-grit paper and moving on to 100-, 120-, and 180-grits. If the top is made of very hard wood such as maple, you may need to use a belt sander for the first pass.

3 Lay the countertop pieces in place and see that they are level, and at the same height where two pieces meet. Add shims as needed. Make sure the top does not wobble.

4 Pull apart two pieces to be joined, and apply a bead of construction adhesive or clear silicone sealer to one of the edges.

7 Apply sealer as recommended by the countertop maker. Avoid stains and chemicals, and look for natural products that will not add toxins to your kitchen—such as mineral oil, linseed oil, or a product made specifically for your top.

Mitered Joint   *TIP*

To make a mitered corner joint like this requires two very long, precise 45-degree cuts. This puts it out of the reach of a do-it-yourselfer. If you want this type of joint, have a wood shop make it for you. They should also router T-slots for installing I-bolts on the underside, as shown on page 137.

6
Sinks and Faucets

Kitchen sinks and faucets get used thousands of times a year, and they are essential elements of a kitchen's appearance. A sink and faucet may recede visually, or they may form a dynamic duo that makes a bold design statement. While some prices are sky high, there are a number of stylish and durable sinks and faucets that won't blow your budget. Replacing a sink or changing a faucet calls for some plumbing work, but you don't need to install new drain or supply lines, so the task is eminently reachable for a do-it-yourselfer. You'll learn all you need to know to replace a sink or faucet, as well as how to install a hot-water dispenser.

Choosing Sinks

A sparkling-clean new sink is an upgrade that will refresh your outlook on cleaning up in the kitchen. You have lots of options; here are some considerations to think about:

- A **double-bowl sink** used to be the norm—one bowl to wash, another to rinse. And you may want one bowl to wash and another for preparing food. But given the heavy reliance on dishwashers, many people today choose a single-bowl sink instead. Or they choose a sink with one large bowl for washing and a small one for rinsing vegetables. Some companies offer cutting boards and colanders that fit right over the sink.
- Make sure your sink is large enough to accommodate your needs. A **standard sink bowl,** 8 or 9 inches deep and 14 or 15 inches square, is enough for plates and average pots, but if you often use large pots you may want to choose a wider and deeper bowl.
- An **under-mount sink** is often preferred because it is easy to wipe crumbs and moist waste into it. A **self-rimming (drop-in) sink** has a rim that gets in the way when wiping. The under-mount option requires a countertop cutout with finished edges; most often, that means a granite or quartz slab countertop and professional installation. Self-rimming sinks, on the other hand, can be installed by do-it-yourselfers onto any countertop.

Today's acrylic sinks, opposite top, are remarkably durable, scrubbable, and lighter in weight than look-alike porcelain.

Stainless-steel sinks, opposite bottom, never go out of style and are hard to beat for durability and cleanability. A self-rimming type is the easiest to install. Cleaning requires wiping around the rim, which you may or may not find irksome.

A geometric design like this, top, may be worth the expense to establish a sleek Euro feel in the kitchen; cook's accessories create versatile work spaces.

This three-compartment arrangement, right, makes it easy to wash, rinse, and dry in three separate bowls. A nestling colander and dish drainer complete the ensemble.

147

■ **Stainless-steel sinks** have great durability and beauty, though dents can be a problem, and some people complain of spotting. Choose a sink that is 20 gauge or less (the lower the gauge, the thicker the steel). It should also have soundproofing foam sprayed onto the underside. Stainless steel rated either "302" or "304" has a good combination of metals (mostly carbon steel, chromium, and molybdenum) to resist rusting and staining.

■ **Enameled cast-iron sinks** have a porcelain-enamel finish and come in a variety of colors. These sinks are heavier, quieter, and more durable than stainless-steel sinks.

■ Sinks made of **copper** are gaining popularity. They tend to be both pricy and high maintenance. But if you love the look and don't mind polishing once a month or so, a copper sink may be for you.

■ **Farmhouse sinks,** also called apron sinks, have decorative front aprons; some have their own backsplash as well. These sinks have a cottage charm and offer a capacious bowl as well. Some rest on top of the countertop, so they are self-rimming, while others installed flush with the countertop. Unless you buy a cabinet made for the sink, installation will require careful custom-cutting of the cabinet as well as the countertop.

This apron sink, above, has holes for mounting a wall faucet, reminiscent of 1930s kitchens but with all the modern conveniences.

A stainless-steel under-mount sink coupled with a quartz countertop, below, makes for easy cleaning and low maintenance.

Buffing a Stainless-Steel Sink

Nothing can repair dents in a stainless-steel sink, and nothing can make an old sink look exactly brand new. But if yours is dingy and covered with minor scratches, try cleaning with a product made for stainless steel. If that doesn't satisfy, buffing can help restore the sink's luster.

At an automobile parts store, purchase a buffing kit with disks and pads that attach to a drill, as well as some liquid buffing compound that is slightly abrasive. Clear the area, and cover nearby walls because you will create a good deal of spatter. Attach the roughest abrasive pad to the drill, and squirt some compound into the sink ❶. Hold the drill with both hands to stabilize it as you polish the bottom ❷. Slowly work upward along the sides; then work on the top rim. Once you have spent 10 minutes or so and have gone over everything at least four times, switch to a gentler buffing pad and repeat ❸. You may need to add buffing compound from time to time. Rinse the sink, which should now be shiny and less scratch-ridden ❹.

Choosing Faucets

Today's faucets are sleek and fashionable, and there is an appealing style to fit any kitchen decor. Even the most outlandish-looking faucets connect to a home's plumbing system in the same way, and this chapter will show how to install them all.

Some faucets will last a long time with no problems, while others may need to be repaired or replaced within a few years. Here are a few tips for finding a faucet that you won't have to worry about for decades:

- In general, very cheap faucets will probably fail sooner than you like. You don't have to pay rich-guy prices, but paying an average or slightly above-average price will likely save you money over the long haul because the faucet will last longer.
- A faucet that feels heavy in your hands has more brass parts than a faucet that is so light it feels like a toy, and it will likely last a good deal longer.
- Open the box, and take a look at the parts: the more plastic you see, the more likely it will fail.
- Brushed stainless steel or nickel costs more than chrome finish, but they will be easier to maintain. Some finishes are "chrome" over plastic and will certainly wear away in time.

You should understand how your faucet will mount onto your sink. A faucet with a flange will likely cover three holes in the sink's deck; if you have a fourth hole, it can be filled with a sprayer, hot-water dispenser, or soap dispenser. Some newer faucets need only one hole; if so, be sure you know how you will fill the other holes. *Widespread* faucets have no flange on top; each component fits into an individual hole.

This faucet's simple sleek boomerang design, opposite top, is a pleasant minimalist choice for a bar sink.

A pot-filler faucet, opposite middle, allows you to fill large pots without carrying them from the sink. Plumbing must be run through the wall, which is not difficult if the wall surface is removed.

Function defines form: a pull-away hose faucet, opposite bottom, has a serious industrial look that feels whimsical in a home kitchen.

Many of today's faucets occupy only one hole in the sink or countertop, for a minimalist look. This faucet, top, has a pullout spout.

At right, the classic four-hole arrangement with separate sprayer is given a new stylistic lease on life. Here, it softens the effect of a rectilinear sink.

Installing Faucets

Many people prefer a traditional faucet that has two
handles and a separate pullout sprayer. Many older spray-
ers were unreliable and stopped spraying after a year or
so, but better-quality models made today are more reliable. Kitchen faucets are usually easy to install; however;
there are three possible snags: **(1)** If the sink is already
installed, reaching the mounting hardware can be difficult. A basin wrench will help. **(2)** Make sure to buy supply
tubes that are long enough to reach your stop valves. If the
faucet comes with supply tubes attached, you may need
to extend them. (See page 153.). **(3)** The connection at the
end of the supply tubes must match the size of your stop
valves—either a ½-inch or ⅜-inch. compression fitting.

This faucet-and-sprayer configuration will fill four holes
in the sink. If your sink has four holes and you would like
a hot-water dispenser, filtered water tap, and/or soap
dispenser, you may choose among other faucet types that
occupy one, two, or three holes.

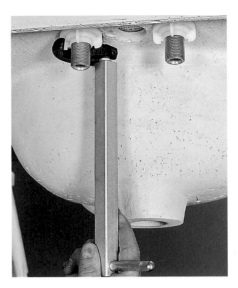

If you are
replacing a
faucet on a sink
that is installed
onto a counter-
top, reaching
the mounting
nuts can be
difficult. A basin
wrench reaches
up into tight
spots, making it
worth its mod-
est cost even if
you only use it
once.

Today many faucets are made to install into a single
hole, which may be in the sink or the countertop. Most do
not require plumber's putty or caulk. Manufacturers have
their own mounting methods, and the one opposite is
one example. Be sure to install the washers in the correct
order, to keep from possibly cracking the sink.

Comfort under the Sink

Working under a sink can be mighty awkward and
even painful, so make things as pleasant as you can.
Spread some thick towels in the cabinet under the
sink to make things comfy, and use a flashlight to help
locate the mounting hardware. So that you don't have
to continually get up and down, place tools in easy
reach, or have a helper stand by to hand them to you.

**Two holes were drilled in the quartz countertop for the
faucet and detergent dispenser shown at right.**

Faucets with Pullout Sprayers

Different faucets install in different ways, but the basics
remain the same: The faucet itself is mounted to holes
in the sink deck or in the countertop, and supply tubes
reach to stop valves in the cabinet below. The model
shown on pages 154–155 has a decorative plate with only
one purpose—to cover two sink holes. If you don't have
extra holes, or if you choose to fill them with a hot-water
dispenser, water filter, or soap dispenser, you won't need
this plate. This faucet has a head that pulls out to become
a sprayer—a very popular feature these days.

Installing a Single-Hole Faucet

• Faucet • Supply tubes, if they are not already attached • Adjustable wrench or groove-joint pliers • Screwdriver

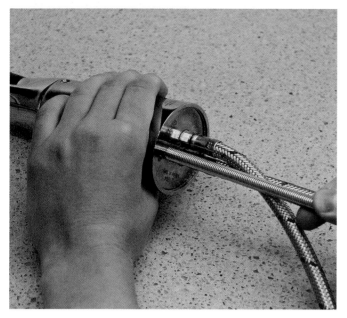

1 Assemble parts onto the faucet. Here, a long threaded rod is screwed in. Attach any rubber O-rings that help seal the faucet base to the counter or sink.

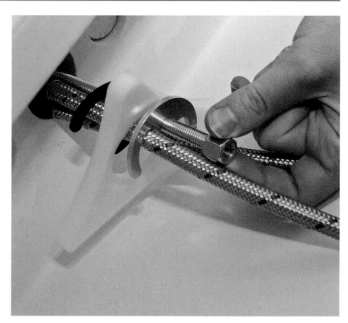

2 Thread the supply tubes through the hole. it might be a tight fit. Have a helper hold the faucet in place as you work from below, and slide on the rubber washer, plastic retaining ring, and metal washer; then screw on the mounting nut.

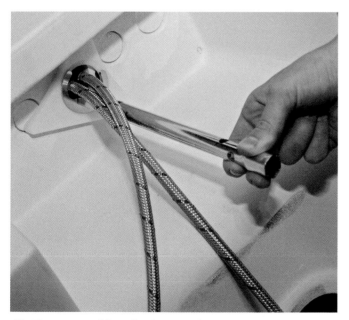

3 Use a screwdriver, basin wrench, or (as in this example) a special wrench provided by the manufacturer to tighten the nut. Make it just snug enough for the faucet to stay in place; then give it another one-quarter turn.

Extending the Supply Tube   TIP

Some newer faucets come with supply tubes already attached. Unfortunately, these tubes are sometimes pretty short. If your supply tubes do not reach your stop valves, go to a home center or hardware store and have a knowledgeable salesperson help you find the right parts for extending yours. Remember that the extension needs to fit your stop valve—either $\frac{1}{2}$-inch or $\frac{3}{8}$-inch compression. In some cases you can simply buy an extension tube that has a male end that fits onto your tubes. In other cases adding a nipple (short pipe that is threaded on each end) will enable you to add on a standard supply tube.

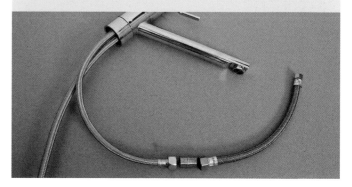

Installing a Faucet with a Pullout Sprayer

• Faucet • Screwdriver • Groove-joint pliers • Latex tub-and-tile caulk • Pipe joint compound • PVC trap and drain line • Supply risers

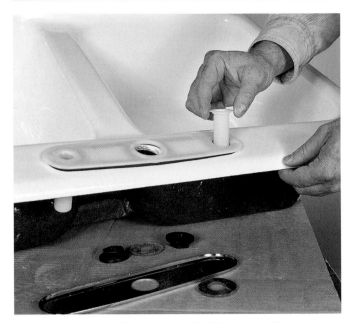

1 Place the base plate over the deck holes, and insert the nuts that hold it in place. Screw on the mounting nuts, and make them finger-tight. If the sink is already installed, you may need to use a basin wrench to reach the nuts. Check that the plate is parallel with the back edge of the sink.

2 Snap the decorative cover onto the base plate. Thread the faucet's supply lines through the middle hole, and insert the faucet body. See that it seats snugly onto the base plate.

5 If it is not already attached, connect the sprayer/spout to the hose, and tighten the fittings. Inside the cabinet below, connect the weight to the bottom of the hose loop; this provides the right amount of tension for moving the sprayer in and out. Test that you can pull the sprayer out and move it back in smoothly.

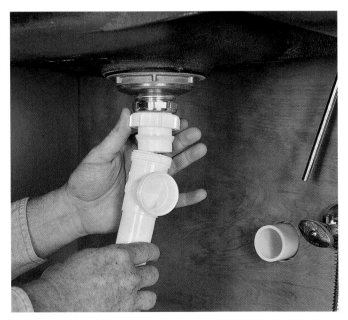

6 If you are installing a new sink, install the basket strainer and the tailpiece; then cut and install the trap parts (and perhaps a waste-disposal unit) as shown on pages 160–165.

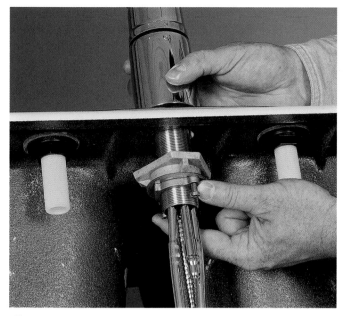

3 Slide the mounting hardware onto the column, and thread the hardware up the shank of the faucet. This model has a plastic spacer, a steel washer, and set screws. Snug the parts up against the faucet, and tighten the screws.

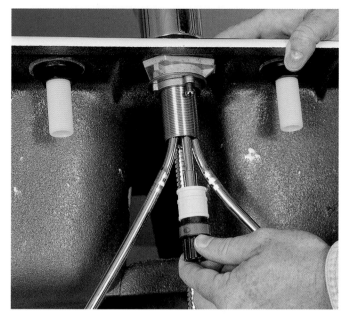

4 Loop the sprayer's hose so it will not snag on any plumbing or other obstructions below, and hook it to the faucet nipple. This unit joins together via a slip fitting with an O-ring seal. Other types screw on. Tighten the attachment.

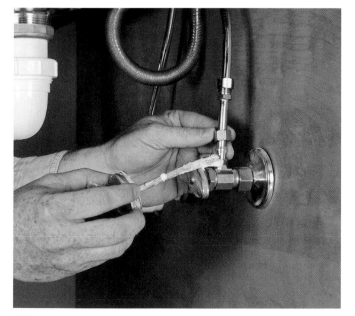

7 You will likely have to attach an extension to the faucet's supply tube(s). Hold the tube in place; mark it; and cut it to length using a tubing cutter. Slide the extension into place between the supply tube and the valve; coat the threads and ferrule on each end with pipe joint compound; and tighten the compression nuts on both ends of the extension tube using an adjustable wrench.

Another Sprayer Option

TIP

Here's a less expensive option that that also provides for flexible spraying. This faucet's spout is attached to a rubber hose. You can remove the spout from its mounting and move it around for spraying. The range of movement is not as large as for a pullout type of faucet, but you will be able to reach every part of the sink.

Hot-Water Dispensers

This handy amenity instantly delivers 200-degree water—hot enough to make tea, prepare instant foods, cook or parboil foods like thin asparagus, and on and on. It's also handy for cleaning hard-to-scrub pots. Of course, a unit with a larger tank will deliver more instant hot water—and will probably cost more. Also take into account the unit's recovery time, measured in how many cups of hot water the dispenser can deliver in an hour.

In order to install one, you must have an electrical receptacle (outlet) under the sink that is always hot (not controlled by a switch). In some setups, the under-sink receptacle is "split and switched" so that one plug is controlled by a switch (for the waste-disposal unit) and one plug is always hot.

Add a Filter? **TIP**

If your water has a metallic, sulfurous, or other "off" taste, it may be advisable for you to add a water filter to the hot-water dispenser. The manufacturer may sell a filter that is easily installed with your unit.

Drilling holes in a countertop is not all that difficult, so plan for as many conveniences as you wish. The sink at right has two soap dispensers, one for hands and one for dishes, in addition to a hot-water dispenser. Another hole has been plugged to allow for a future upgrade. (The cylindrical object is a dishwasher air gap, required by some plumbing codes.)

Meeting Code

The project opposite calls for installing a saddle valve, which does not meet code in some areas. For a compliant connection, replace a cold-water stop valve with one that has two outlets, and connect the supply pipe to that. Be sure to shut off the water to the house before removing the old stop valve.

Installing a Hot-Water Dispenser

• Hot-water dispenser • Saddle valve or split stop valve • Drill-driver • Groove-joint pliers or adjustable wrench

1 Mount the tank in a convenient location under the sink. Make sure the vent and supply tubes from the unit's spout can reach the tank, and plan the path for the water supply line. See that you can plug the unit into an always-hot receptacle.

2 To supply water to the tank, install a saddle T valve onto a nearby cold-water pipe. (Some municipalities frown on this type of valve; see "Meeting Code," on page 156) To install the valve, shut off water to the pipe. Attach the clamps, with a rubber washer, to a copper pipe. Then tighten the valve's handle.

3 Run ¼-in. flexible copper or plastic supply tube from the tank to the valve. Slip on a nut and a ferrule; then insert the end of the tube into the valve. Slide the ferrule over into the valve; then slide and tighten the nut.

7 Thread the spout's tubes through a hole in the sink or countertop. Have a helper hold it in position as you work from below to slide on the mounting washer; then slide and tighten the mounting nut. You may need to use a basin wrench to tighten the nut.

8 Attach three lines to the tank: the water supply from the cold-water valve, and the vent and supply lines from the spout. Depending on the model, these lines may attach using clamps or a push-on connection.

9 Turn on the water supply. Allow time for the water to heat up, and test the unit. Most models allow you to adjust the temperature using a simple dial knob.

Self-Rimming Sinks

While preparing a countertop and installing an under-mount sink is usually best left to the pros, a motivated do-it-yourselfer can certainly tackle a self-rimming sink. Here we show a stainless-steel sink, but an enameled cast-iron sink installs in much the same way—though usually without any mounting clips. If you are installing a new countertop, see pages 119–120.

To remove an existing self-rimming sink, see page 118. Check that the new sink will fit into the existing hole; if not, you may need to widen the hole or buy another sink. Scrape away any caulk or plumber's putty around the hole, and clean with mineral spirits or degreaser. Test to make sure that the new sink will fit.

These steps show a double-bowl sink with a waste-disposal unit, which is a common arrangement. If your sink has only one bowl or if it has no disposal unit, plumbing will be simpler. If you are replacing an existing sink with the same plumbing configuration, mimic the old plumbing when you install the new. You could attach the sink to the countertop first and then install all the plumbing, but here we show installing most of the plumbing first, with the sink upside-down on a pair of sawhorses or the countertop because it is easier.

Follow Local Codes

The following pages show a very common way to hook up a drain for a double-bowl sink. However, local codes may vary. For instance, some building inspectors may require separate P-traps for each sink bowl, with a Y-fitting fitting at the wall to accommodate two trap arms. If you are unsure of plumbing requirements in your area, consult with an inspector or a plumber.

Enameled cast-iron sinks, like the black one shown above, are durable and come in colors that can perk up a kitchen.

If you have a wood countertop, below, a self-rimming sink is a safer option because it keeps the end grain of the wood from direct water exposure.

Installing a Self-Rimming Sink

• Self-rimming sink, with mounting clips • Waste-disposal unit • Trap and other pieces, or a disposal-unit install kit
• Plumber's putty • Groove-joint pliers • Appliance cord or electrical cable • Saw for cutting trap pieces • Silicone caulk • Screwdriver

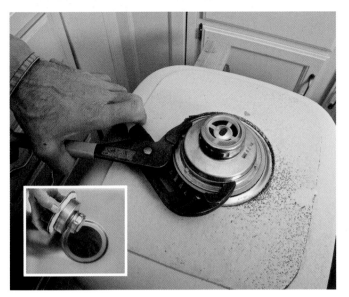

1 Install the basket strainer for the bowl that does not have a disposer. Apply a rope of putty to the underside of a strainer flange (inset); push it into place; then hold it still while you slip on the washers and tighten the large nut. A large pair of groove-joint pliers works fine for this, though a spud wrench (which you may use only once or twice in your life) is easier to use.

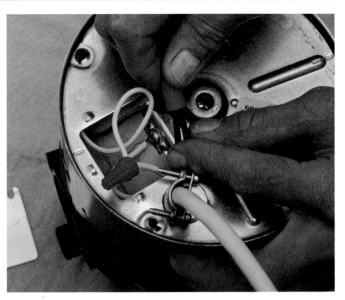

2 Prepare the disposal unit for installation. If you will plug it into a receptacle, use an appliance cord, as shown. If the unit will be hard-wired to an electrical box, shut off power to the circuit, and wire it directly to the box, as shown on page 165.

3 If you will run the dishwasher drain hose to the waste-disposal unit, use a hammer and screwdriver to remove the knockout inside the unit's drain inlet. Install the unit's basket strainer as shown for the other strainer (Step 1). Follow manufacturer's instructions for assembling the mounting hardware. You will need to slip on a tightly fitting ring to hold it together.

4 Place the waste-disposal unit onto the strainer, and turn the mounting nut to fasten it firmly. You can now rotate the unit as needed.

Continued on next page

Installing a Self-Rimming Sink, cont'd.

5 Temporarily attach a tailpiece and the T-fitting to the other bowl, and attach the straight arm that runs from the waste-disposal unit; it will be too long at this point. The straight arm must be straight or slightly sloped downward (upward as you look at it upside down). Measure the tailpiece for how much you need to cut for the downward slope.

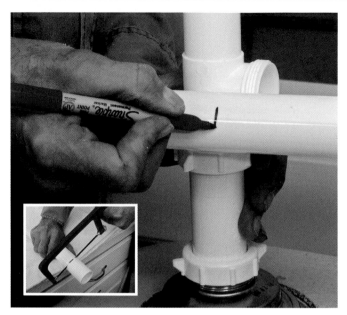

6 To cut trap pieces, use a power miter saw, miter saw, or hacksaw (inset). Hold the pipe firmly as you cut. After cutting, scrape the inside and outside of the cut to remove any burrs. Install the shortened tailpiece, and measure for cutting the straight arm that runs to the T-fitting. The arm should insert most of the way into the fitting.

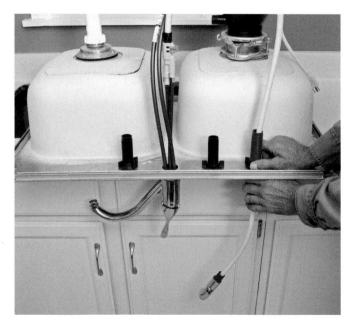

9 Install the faucet, as well as any sprayer, hot-water dispenser, soap dispenser, or water-filter spout. See pages 152-57 for faucet-installation tips.

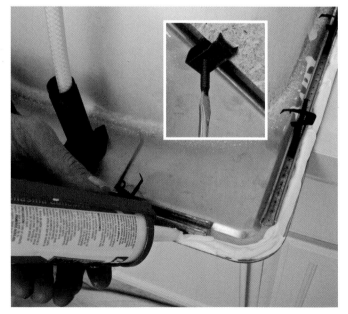

10 Slide mounting clips into the sink's channels. (Here, the clips are black; other types may look different.) Apply a thick bead of silicone caulk under the flange. Working with a helper. Lower the sink carefully into the hole. You may need to adjust mounting clips so they don't get in the way. While the helper holds the sink in position above, crawl below and tighten the clips to hold the sink firmly in place (inset).

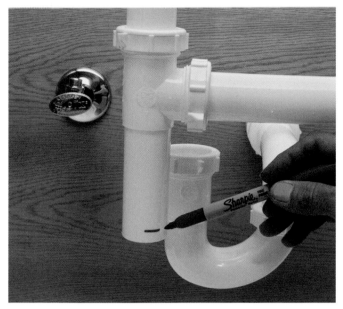

7 Temporarily install the trap into the trap fitting in the wall. Set the sink temporarily in the hole, making sure its rim rests on the countertop. From below, measure for cutting the lower tailpiece. After cutting, the horizontal arm that runs to the wall should be sloped downward. Again, measure so the tailpiece inserts most of the way into the trap fitting.

8 You may need to cut the arm running to the wall. Set the sink back on the sawhorses or table, and attach the entire trap assembly. Plastic trap pieces like these can be tightened firmly by hand. Make sure all fittings are assembled with plastic washers as well as nuts. Do not fully tighten the nuts below the tailpiece at this time

11 Use paper towels, then a solvent-soaked rag, to wipe away squeezed-out silicone caulk from around the sink's flange. If you see any places where the flange is not resting firmly on the countertop, go below and tighten a clip. You may need to add another clip or two.

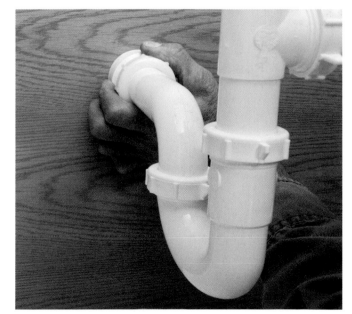

12 From below, insert the trap arm into the trap adapter in the wall, and tighten all the nuts. Attach the faucet's supply tubes to the stop valves. Plug-in or wire the disposal unit. Restore power and water, and test for leaks by filling the bowls and then removing the stoppers.

Farmhouse Sinks

Also called an apron sink, farmhouse sinks have various shapes. Some incorporate a backsplash, and some have drainer shelves. Most have aprons in front and are wide enough to reach to the back wall, which means that there is no narrow strip of countertop at the front or back. Some install in an under-mount configuration, while others (like the one shown opposite) have a rim that rests on top of the countertop.

Because of size and shape of the sink, you will probably need to cut your sink base cabinet and add extra support pieces. Be sure to understand how the sink should be supported. For instance, the model opposite is supported by its rim, which rests on the countertop, but the manufacturer recommends adding clips for further support.

A simply elegant single-bowl white apron sink, above, complements almost any decor and offers plenty of versatility when washing and rinsing. A single large bowl is popular with people who do most of their dinnerware cleanup in the dishwasher.

The enameled sink shown at left features old-fashioned designs that will not fade over time and do not cause cleaning difficulties.

Below, a stainless-steel apron sink offers a distinctive gleaming vertical surface. The wood countertop's exposed edges must be kept meticulously well sealed.

Installing a Rimming Apron Sink

• Self-rimming apron sink • Silicone caulk • Solvent and rag • Support clips or wood bracing

1 Here, a sink base cabinet is prepared for a self-rimming farmhouse sink with its left rim at the end of the counter (so there is no countertop to the left of the sink). The base's false drawers were removed, and the framing was cut to accommodate the front apron. The countertop is square cut, and the backsplash is installed; the sink's rim will fit over the top and will butt against the backsplash.

2 Test to be sure that the sink will fit. Attach the faucet and drain plumbing as you would for a self-rimming sink. (See pages 158–161.) Apply a bead of silicone caulk to the edge of the countertop, and set the sink in it. Use a solvent-dampened rag to wipe away excess silicone.

3 If needed, install support clips below the sink, which may be supplied by the sink manufacturer. Or install wood bracing.

Attaching an Under-Mount Sink

To attach an under-mount sink, the fabricator drills holes around the sink basin from below. Threaded rods are inserted into the holes and held in place with epoxy adhesive. After the epoxy dries, the sink can be mounted. A bead of silicone caulk is applied to the top of the sink's rim to form a watertight seal against the bottom of the countertop. The sink is pressed into place and is held in place by tightening clips.

Waste-Disposal Units

A waste-disposal unit greatly eases the task of rinsing pots and pans because you don't have to clean away bits of food; instead, just send them down the drain and turn on the unit. Check to be sure that a waste-disposal unit is allowed in your area, however: they are forbidden in some locales, especially where septic systems are in use.

Replacing an existing disposal unit often requires no changes to your existing plumbing, as long as you purchase a unit of the same make and model. In many cases, you can even upgrade, say, from a ⅓-horsepower model to one that pulls a full horsepower without plumbing changes. Take your old unit to the store, and hold it next to the new one to see whether trap plumbing will need to be modified or not.

If you are installing a waste-disposal unit where none exists, you will need to change the trap. See pages 160–163 for one way to hook up the drain. Also understand how it will be wired: a *continuous feed* unit is turned on and off by a switch on the wall or cabinet. That means that there must be an electrical box or receptacle inside the cabinet that is controlled by a switch. If you have an under-cabinet receptacle that is always hot, you can plug in a *batch feed* unit. It turns on when you insert a special stopper into the unit's strainer and turn it.

Removing an Existing Waste-Disposal Unit

If the disposal unit is hard-wired to a box, shut off power at the service panel. If it is plugged into a receptacle, unplug it. Loosen the hose clamp, and remove the dishwasher hose, if there is one. Disconnect the trap arm ❶, inset. Use a screwdriver to turn the retainer ring counterclockwise until it is loose, Support the disposer with your other hand, and allow it to drop down ❶.

Remove the disposal unit's electrical coverplate, and disconnect the wires and the cable. (See step 4, opposite page.) To remove the basket strainer, loosen the three bolts that hold the retaining ring in place ❷, inset. Then pry out the snap ring with the tip of a flat-blade screwdriver ❷. Now you can easily remove the other parts (gaskets and mounting flange).

Installing a Waste-Disposal Unit

• Waste-disposal unit • Plumber's putty • Screwdriver • Appliance cord or electrical cable • Wire stripper
• Tool for cutting trap parts • Groove-joint pliers

1 From above, place a rope of plumber's putty around the drain flange and insert it into the sink hole. Have a helper hold it in place as you work from below to install the mounting assembly. Lift the cardboard gasket, the metal gasket, the mounting flange, and the split ring up over the flange. Snap the ring into the depression at the bottom of the strainer; then tighten the mounting flange's bolts (inset).

2 Remove the unit's electrical cover plate after loosening its screws. Remove 6 in. of sheathing from an appliance cord or cable; slide the wires into the unit; and clamp the cable or cord. Strip wire ends as needed, and attach the grounding wire to the grounding screw. Splice the white and black wires using wire connectors, and replace the cover plate.

3 Lift the disposal unit up into position, and rotate the mounting ring until it fits over the flange. (If the unit is heavy, you may need a helper for this. Or rest the disposal unit on a temporary support so that you don't have to lift it very far.) Use a screwdriver to tighten the ring.

4 If you will run a dishwasher hose to the waste-disposal unit, use a hammer and screwdriver to remove the knockout plug inside the drain inlet. Install the trap's drain line to the side of the unit. (See pages 160-161.) Push the dishwasher hose onto the unit's drain inlet, and tighten a clamp to secure it (inset). Plug-in or wire the unit.

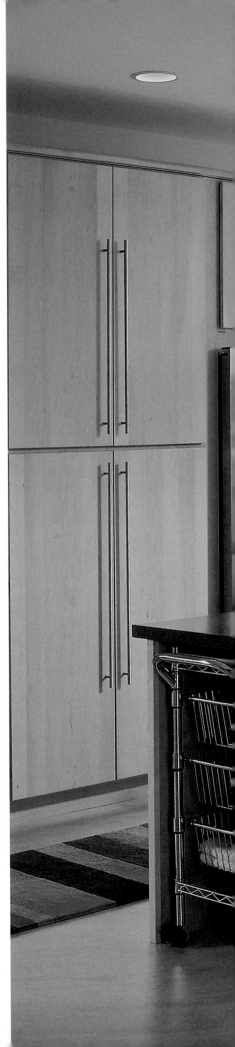

7

Lighting & Electrical Upgrades

A simple change of light fixtures can dramatically enhance the look of a kitchen. Of course, stronger lighting will make it a brighter, cheerier place, but specific types of lights, carefully placed, can give you a new perspective on your kitchen, highlighting work areas and tables, or simply providing even light throughout the entire room. This chapter will show how to install all the basic types of lighting. Most of the lighting projects do not call for running new electrical cable; you can install them onto ceiling boxes or other wiring that already exists.

You may be surprised to learn how easy it is to replace a dishwasher, range hood, or cooktop. In most kitchens, the wiring and plumbing is already in place for these appliances, and replacement usually takes less than half a day.

Planning Kitchen Lighting

According to real estate experts, people often complain that a kitchen is too dark, making it dreary in the evenings. While a low level of light can be soothing in other rooms in the home, a goodly supply of overhead and focused work light makes the food prep easier and more pleasant, and makes your kitchen a happier place. Light fixtures can also add zest to the overall design of a kitchen. This can be a subtle effect—with recessed ceiling lights or under-cabinet lights, for instance—which don't call attention to themselves. Lights that are highly visible or even dangle down, like pendant, track, or cable lights, can help tie the look of the kitchen together while they add their own special sparkle.

Most kitchens need several types of lighting. It might seem like too much if you had everything switched on at the same time, but an overall ambient light that evenly lights the whole room, together with numerous focused lights to illuminate work areas, are usually needed to satisfy chefs and kitchen visitors.

Overhead light usually comes from ceiling fixtures, including recessed lights and track lights, but it may also come from cabinet up-lights or sconces. Even on a dark overcast day, adequate ambient light will make your kitchen feel warm and welcoming. If your kitchen has high ceilings, you may need brighter lights. If your kitchen has white cabinets, which reflect light, you may get away with less lighting.

For work areas, experts recommend focused light at the 100-watt level, (or 60 watts of fluorescent light). If you don't have this level of light in your work areas, upgrading your lighting will enhance the pleasure of cooking, cleaning, and reading recipes. Under-cabinet lights are a popular, effective option for lighting a countertop. You'll want the same level of light over the sink and cooktop, too.

Choosing Light Fixtures

For overhead ambient light, most of us are used to the soft warm glow of incandescent bulbs, but the US and Canadian governments are phasing them out. (The reason is that the bulbs use 90 percent of their energy generating heat and only 10 percent in providing light.) Compact fluorescent lamps (CFLs), known for a cooler blue light, have improved in recent years, and they are energy efficient inasmuch as they use only 13 watts to provide the equivalent of 60 watts of incandescent illumination.

LED (light-emitting diode) bulbs are expensive but are becoming popular workhorses in energy-efficient kitchens, especially for task, track, and recessed lights. Using less electricity, they provide bright light and last many years longer than incandescent bulbs—and let off less heat.

- **Flush ceiling fixtures** (which have a canopy that hugs the ceiling) provide ambient light for a room, directing light both up toward the ceiling and down toward the room.
- **Pendants**—lights that hang down—provide stylish task lighting; they are usually adjustable for height. Chandeliers (pendants with multiple bulbs) are fairly uncommon in a kitchen.
- **Recessed lights** cast light down for brighter and more even ambient lighting. They have a clean, trim look.
- **Track lights** provide precise focused light. You can choose the voltage, location, and direction of each light, and choose from a wide array of lengths, shapes, and styles.
- **Under-cabinet lights** provide bright task lighting without shining into the eyes of the person working at the counter. They gently brighten up a room. They are needed because with only overhead lighting, the cook's body will make a shadow.

In the kitchen opposite, recessed canister lights provide general illumination; three perfectly placed pendants light up the island countertop; and the range hood's light illuminates the cooktop.

Low-voltage Euro-style pendants, top left, are arranged along a rectangular hanging track positioned above a table.

This low-voltage light track, left, can be easily bent into a curve that suits the room. The lower-hanging pendants can attach to ceiling boxes or to the track.

Four Types of Lighting

Total kitchen lighting is the result of at least three, and often four, types of lights.

- **Ambient,** or **general, lighting** is the starting point or foundation. It usually comes from recessed or flush ceiling lights, which provide an even, diffuse level of light for the room. But a combination of accent, task, and decorative lighting can also help provide an overall ambient effect.

- **Task lighting** directs focused light just where you need it—most commonly above counters, sinks, and cooktops. It's considered another layer of light that supplements the ambient light, which is not bright enough for specific work sections.

- **Accent light** is a layer of light aimed at a certain feature of a room to make it more noticeable. Several types of light can be used for this effect, including track lights, spot lights, or sconces. The beam pattern and light intensity can vary depending on the bulb you choose. Halogen bulbs are more intense.

- **Decorative light fixtures** provide a focal point for the room; they add character and sparkle.

Yellow pendant lights, left, are only one of the hundreds of styles from which you can choose. They are available at home centers or from online sources.

Extra-bulbous black shades on pendant lights, opposite top, create light that is focused but wide enough for the table; under-cabinet lights highlight the sunny-yellow backsplash tiles.

Working Safely with Electricity

When it comes to wiring, safer is always better. Electricity may be scary stuff, but if you follow these three steps you'll ensure against any shocking experiences:

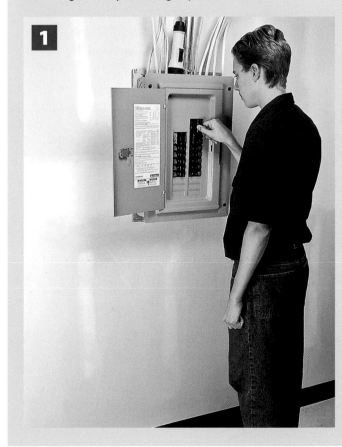

To shut off power, find your service panel and flip off the breaker (or remove the fuse, if you have an old fuse box) that controls the circuit you are working on ❶. If the panel does not have a list telling you which breaker covers which areas of the house, you may have to keep flipping breakers until you find the right one. Lock the service panel, or at least leave a large note telling people not to turn the power back on.

Then test. If you are working on a receptacle, insert the probes of a tester into both outlets to be sure ❷. If you are working on a light, turn on the switch to verify that the light does not come on. Then, when you have removed the light fixture, test the wire ends with a voltage tester to be sure.

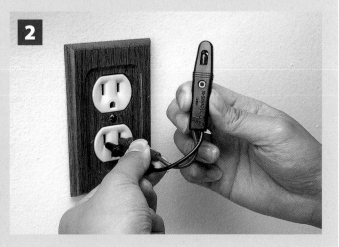

Ceiling-Mounted Fixtures

A ceiling-mounted, or flush, fixture has a canopy that snugs up against the ceiling. The fixture may be simple, with one bulb and a globe, or it may have several bulbs with globes, but the wiring is essentially the same.

If possible, choose a new fixture whose canopy is as large or larger than the old one. If the new one is smaller, you may need to patch and paint the ceiling around it. Most light fixtures come with all of the hardware you need for installation.

Be Safe

Before removing the old fixture, shut off power at the service panel . Depending on the type of wiring, simply turning off the light switch may—or may not—shut off all power to the ceiling box, and there's no sense taking chances.

This simply elegant ceiling fixture with minimal hardware manages to draw little attention to itself as it quietly does its job.

Center-Mount Fixtures

If your fixture attaches to the electrical box via a threaded nipple, you may need to attach a new strap with a threaded hole in its middle. Screw the center nipple up into the strap ❶. Wire the fixture as shown on the following page. Slip the fixture canopy up so that the nipple pokes through, and screw on a mounting nut ❷.

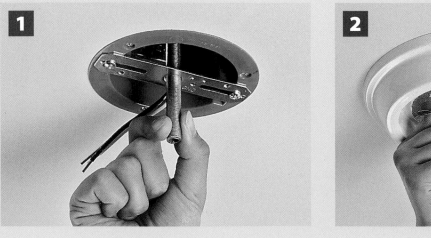

Replacing a Ceiling-Mounted Fixture

• Voltage tester • Screwdriver • Wire strippers • Light fixture

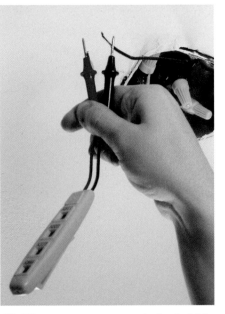

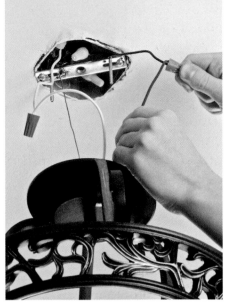

1 Loosen the screws that hold the globe in place, and remove the globe (top). Remove two screws that hold the canopy in place, or loosen them enough so you can twist and remove the canopy. If the fixture has a center nut, remove it. Pull down the canopy (bottom).

2 Disconnect any ground wire (which is either green or bare copper). Spread apart the white and black (or colored) wires. Remove the wire nuts, and gently pull off the fixture's wires (which are called leads). Test to be sure there is no power in the ceiling wires.

3 If the existing hardware does not match the new canopy, install a strap, as needed. Attach the fixture's ground lead to a screw in the box, or splice it to the house's ground wire. Splice the fixture's white and black leads to the house's white and black wires.

4 Carefully fold the wires back up into the box (inset). Start driving two mounting screws into the holes in the strap. Push the canopy up so that the screws poke through the larger portion of the holes, twist the canopy, and drive the screws to snug the canopy against the ceiling.

5 Following the manufacturer's instructions, screw in lightbulbs, and add the canopy or other coverings. Restore power, and test.

Pendant Fixtures

A pendant fixture hangs down. (If a pendant has a number of individual bulbs, it is called a chandelier.) There are a number of mounting methods for pendants; here we show the most common. In all cases, the light's wires need to pass through a threaded nipple, which may be attached to the box via a strap or a device called a hickey. Some track lighting fixtures have pendants that can attach to them. (See pages 178–179.)

First, determine the desired height of the light. If the pendant is over a dining table or counter, it may be installed at a height of 60 inches or so from the floor, depending on the type of light. If the pendant will hang where people will walk beneath it, it should be no lower than 76 inches. The best way to determine the correct height is to temporarily attach the light and see how comfortable people are with it.

Yellow pendants, above, seem like upside-down wine glasses with extra-long stems.

The foreground chandelier below is matched in style by the three pendants over the island.

Pendant with Rod or Cable

This type of pendant light has a cord that also supports the light, so there is no need for a chain. Installation is very similar to installing a flush light: cut the cord the desired hanging distance plus 6 inches; strip off the cord's sheathing; and wire the cord to the house wires. Slip the canopy up; attach it to the cord; and attach the canopy to the ceiling box via two mounting screws.

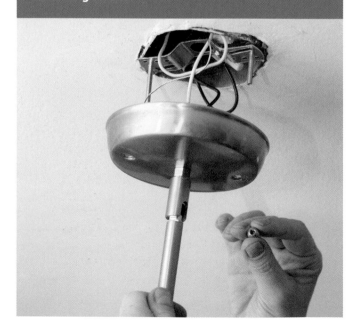

Installing a Pendant Fixture

• Voltage tester • Screwdriver • Pendant fixture • Wire cutters • Wire connectors

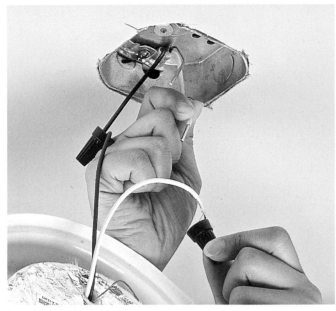

1 Shut off power to the circuit, and test that power is off. Remove or loosen the existing fixture's mounting screws; pull down the canopy; and disconnect the wiring.

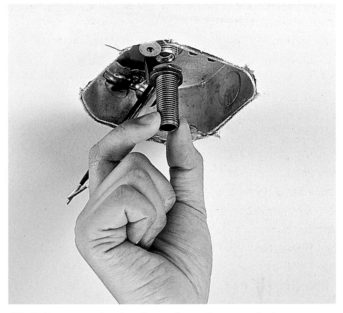

2 Using mounting hardware from the manufacturer, install a threaded nipple into a strap or hickey. (A hickey is shown.) There must be room above the threaded nipple for wiring to pass through. Cut the pendant's chain to the desired length, and slip the mounting nut and canopy over the chain.

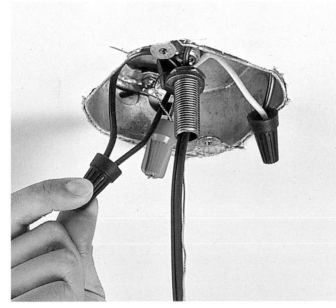

3 Support the pendant light with a stepladder, or have someone hold it as you work. Thread the pendant's lead wires through the nipple. Screw the ground lead to a grounding screw in the box, or splice it to a grounding wire. Connect the black and white leads to the black and white house wires.

4 Fold the wires back into the box. Slide the canopy up against the ceiling. Slide the mounting nut up, and screw it onto the threaded nipple. Tighten to snug the canopy against the ceiling.

Track Lighting

Track lighting offers tremendous versatility and allows you to totally revamp your overall lighting scheme without disruption to the walls and ceiling by having to run new cables or install new electrical boxes. Starting at a single ceiling box, tracks can branch off in several directions and take any number of turns. You can position one or more tracks in the middle of the kitchen, or run them around the perimeter. (Track lighting will not by itself adequately light a countertop, however, because a person working at the counter would create a shadow on the counter; only under-cabinet lighting can properly light a counter for working.) Once the tracks are installed, you have two more ways to be versatile: the individual lamps can be positioned anywhere along the track, and once positioned, they can be pointed in the direction you choose.

Visit a home center or lighting store to choose the tracks and lamps. You may end up buying individual pieces or a kit that has all the parts you need. Most systems have two possible track lengths, plus L-fittings for turning corners and T-fittings for branching out. You'll also need a floating connecter to connect to the box (attached anywhere along a track's length) or a live-end connector (which attaches at the end of a track). For a complicated track configuration, some companies also offer 45-degree L-fittings, crosses, and even flexible connectors for turning at unusual angles.

A modestly curved track, above left, sports both pointable swivel lights and hanging pendants.

Some newer "Euro" style track lights have tracks that can curve in a tight radius (above right). Some come with the curves already made, while others are flexible so you can create your own sinewy lines. Many of these units feature low-voltage lamps.

If positioned about 12 in. out from wall cabinets, right, track lights can light up the cabinet interiors, as well as a counter below.

Some track systems, opposite, allow you to install hanging pendant lights, with a variety of colored shades or globes. The lamp heights can be adjusted.

Installing Track Lights

• Screwdriver • Voltage tester • Measuring straightedge, pencil • Stud finder • Power connector with cover • Wire connectors

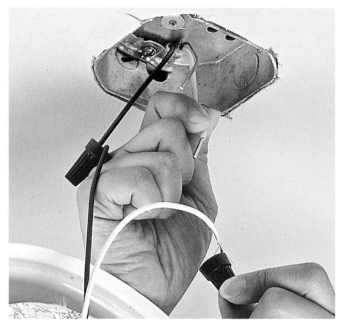

1 Shut off power at the service panel, and test to verify that power is off. Remove the existing ceiling light fixture. (See page 174.) Test again to make sure power is off. Disconnect the wiring.

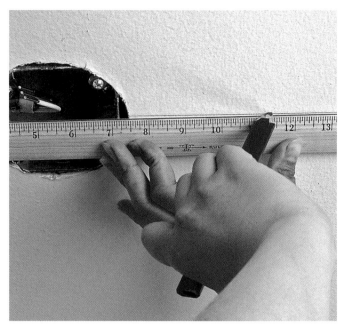

2 Measure and draw guidelines for the placement of the tracks. It often works best to measure out from the nearest wall in two places and draw a line that is parallel with the wall. Use a stud finder to locate joists, and mark their locations.

5 Push the electrical connector into the track, and twist-lock it in place. (Your parts may look different, but the principle is the same; the track connects to the plate, and a connector attaches to the connector in such a way as to energize the track.) Snap the canopy cover in place.

6 Attach the track(s) to the ceiling. If possible, attach it using screws driven into joists. If a track runs parallel with the joists, attach it using toggle bolts or other drywall anchors. Attach end caps at the ends of tracks. Also install T- or L-connectors where needed.

• Wire strippers • Track lights • Fittings as needed • Drill • Screws and toggle bolts

3 Thread wires from the power connector through the mounting plate holes. Connect the connector's ground lead wire to a grounding screw in the box or to a house ground wire. Splice the white and black leads to the house's white and black (or colored) wires; cap with wire connectors.

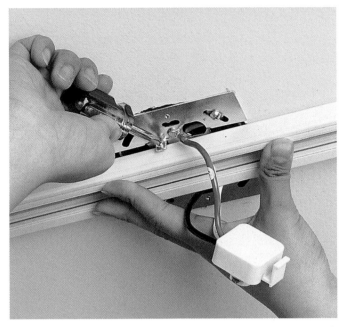

4 Screw the power connector plate to the electrical box. If the box does not have a metal strap with holes correctly spaced for your connector, install a new strap. Lift up a track section, and attach it to the plate.

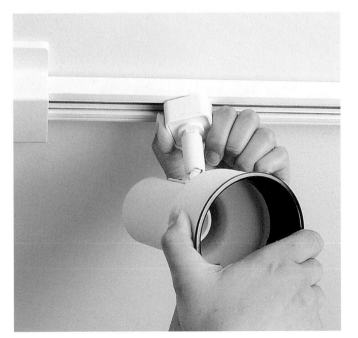

7 Slip a lamp's electrical connector into the track where you want it, and twist to make a firm electrical connection. Most lamps can be swiveled to point where you want them to provide illumination. Install bulbs; restore power; and test the lights.

Recessed Canister Lighting

Recessed lights offer the lowest profile and so are a good choice if you don't want to draw attention to the light fixtures or if you want a lot of lights. You can choose among "cans" with plain trim rings and visible bulbs or models that have a variety of reflectors, baffles, and bulb-covering lenses. Some "eyeball" models swivel so you can point them where you want to provide light. Because installing recessed lighting calls for running new cable, you may want to hire an electrician to do the job.

Cable Lights

Also called trapeze lights, cable lights offer whimsical but effective lighting for small areas. You may consider installing them over a sink, for instance. They come in a kit with a fixture box that has a transformer, so the cables carry only very low voltage, making them safe. These instructions show connecting with surface wiring (also called raceway wiring), but you may choose to hire an electrician to install a switched electrical box on the wall—or do it yourself if you have the skills.

These cable lights use a single cable, which carries both hot and neutral wires.

Installing Cable Lights

- Screwdriver • Voltage tester • Drill • Wire strippers • Wire
- Surface-mounted conduit and wires

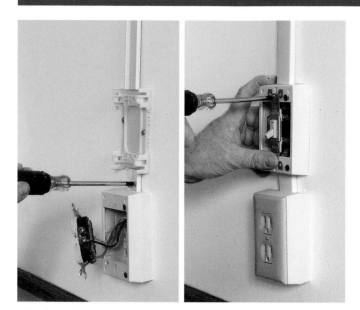

1 Shut off power to the circuit, and test to verify that power is off. Mount a surface-wiring (raceway) box over a standard receptacle; then attach a switch box base and surface conduit to the wall. Run cable from the receptacle box to the switch box, then from the switch box to the cable lights above. Join the wires to the switch, and screw on cover plates.

4 Attach the cable to the holder using threaded fittings (top). Finger tighten these fittings; then snug them tight with pliers. Install cable holders on the opposite wall or cabinet. Hang a turnbuckle adjuster onto both holders (bottom). Attach the cable fittings to the turnbuckles.

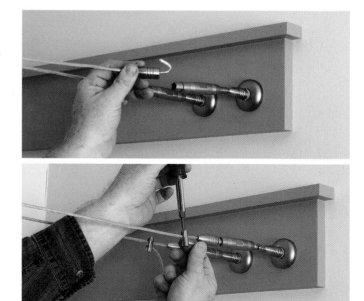

5 Following manufacturer's instructions, attach cables that run between the holders, and tighten the turnbuckles until the cables are taut (top). Attach the short cables that run to the transformer, using self-piercing hardware that makes an electrical connection when you tighten a screw (bottom).

connectors • Surface-mounted receptacle, receptacle, switch, and light boxes
• Cable light kit with cables, lamps, transformer, and mounting hardware

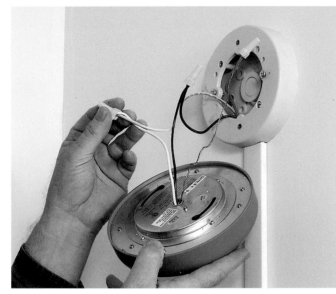

2 Install a surface-mounted light fixture box on the wall near where the cable lights will be installed. Join the cable from the switch below to the fixture transformer's leads. Attach the transformer to the box.

3 Attach cable holders to the wall (or cabinet) by driving the screws provided. If there is no firm surface to which you can attach the holders, use toggle bolts or heavy-duty drywall anchors. (See page 80.)

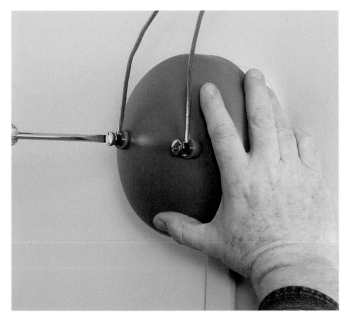

6 Attach the short cables to the terminals on the front of the transformer. Loosen the screws; feed each wire into the respective slot; and tighten the screws to make solid electrical connections.

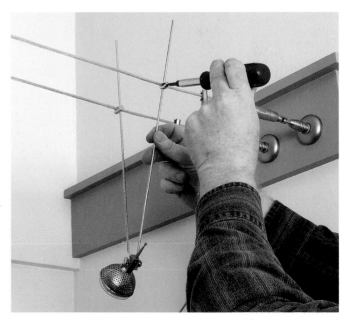

7 Mount each light on the cables using self-piercing fittings. Once attached, the lights can be pointed in different directions. To slide a light over, loosen the screws first; slide; then tighten again.

Under-Cabinet Lighting

Most kitchens already have some kind of under-cabinet lighting that is controlled by a wall switch. Special under-cabinet fluorescent lights, usually only 1 or 1½ inches thick, have long been the most common types. But halogen strips and round "puck" lights are increasingly popular.

Correctly placed under-cabinet lights amply illuminate the work surface without shining in your eyes.

Changing Fixtures

If you have existing fluorescent lighting and just want to change the fixtures, shut off power at the service panel. Remove the diffuser, which just snaps in place. Remove the tube; then loosen and remove the electrical cover, which may be held in place by screws or may just snap into place. At this point you can unscrew the wire connectors and disconnect the wiring. Loosen the two screws that hold the fixture in place, and remove the unit. To install a new fixture, clamp the cable; screw the body to the cabinet; and splice the wires. Attach the canopy screw in the tube, and test the fixture.

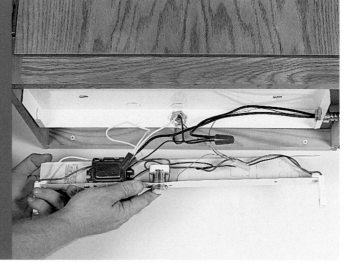

Installing New Hard-Wired Fixtures

If you have no under-cabinet lights and want new ones that are controlled by a wall switch, hire an electrician to run the cables for both the lights and a switch. Local codes may require armored (metal) cable or conduit, or nonmetallic cable may be allowed. An electrician can usually fish cable through walls and the back of the cabinet ❶, or run cable along the underside or the inside of a cabinet, where it is not highly visible. Power must be run from a nearby receptacle or a new circuit in the service panel to a switch ❷, and then on to the light fixtures.

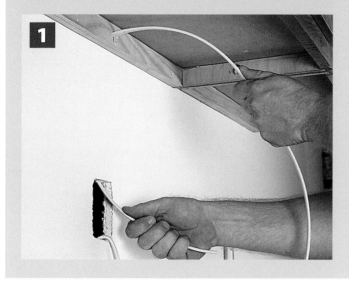

Low-Voltage Halogens

If you have no existing lights and don't want to hire an electrician or run new cable, consider low-voltage halogen lights, often available in kit form. These are available in puck shape or in strips. They are inexpensive and easy to install, and the lights are attractive. The drawbacks: you will control them by using a cord switch or individual switches on the lights rather than a wall switch; some of the wiring will be exposed; and they tend to get fairly hot.

A halogen kit ❶ includes the lights, cords, transformer, and plugs. Attach the lights where you want them. Attach the transformer inside a cabinet or in another inconspicuous place, and run its cord to a wall receptacle. The cord will almost certainly be extra long, so if you have a length of any kind left over after plugging it in, bundle the loose part with twisties and tuck it away. Run the little cords from the lights to the transformer, and plug them in.

The finished installation will have some exposed cords, but they can usually be run inconspicuously ❷. If wiring will be exposed, consider running it through wire covers, which can be painted ❸.

Managing Electrical Circuits

If you are planning to install a new appliance, such as a hot-water dispenser or dishwasher, it's a good idea to do a little figuring to make sure you will not overload a circuit and need to add another. And if you have an older kitchen, its electrical circuits may not be up to the task of powering all your existing appliances.

You may find that a circuit overloads when you use several appliances at once. When this happens, the appliances or lights will go out, and you must go to the service panel and restore power by flipping a circuit breaker (or in the case of a very old system, replacing a fuse).

Modern kitchens are neatly divided with separate circuits for the lights, each major appliance, and two or more circuits for the countertop receptacles. However, a circuit in an older kitchen may supply power to the lights, an appliance, and some receptacles. Electrical codes have gotten stricter and stricter over the years, meaning that an older kitchen is almost certainly not up to current code. If you do a complete kitchen renovation, you will have to bring things up to code. If you are only doing simple work, however, you are usually not required to do so.

Two Things You Can Do before Calling in an Electrician

A circuit that periodically overloads is a problem that needs to be addressed. You may need to call in a professional electrician to install a new circuit or two. But first, there are some steps you may want to take yourself.

- The simplest solution: flip off the breaker on the circuit that often blows, and test to see whether any nearby receptacles are still energized or not. If so, simply plug one or more appliances into those receptacles.
- Many newer appliances use less electricity than older models. This is especially true of microwaves but also applies to toasters, toaster ovens, dishwashers, and other appliances. Replacing an appliance or two may solve your problem.

What an Electrician Can Do

An electrician may want to dig in and rewire your entire kitchen, but first consider simpler solutions.

- You may need only one or two new receptacles that are on a new circuit.
- It may be possible to rewire an existing receptacle or two so they are on a new circuit.
- It's possible to "split" a receptacle (or group of receptacles) so that each of its two plugs is on a different circuit. That way, you can plug two heavy electrical users into the same receptacle.
- If a certain appliance, such as a hot-water dispenser or dishwasher, is on a circuit that overloads, it is often possible to wire that appliance to its own dedicated circuit.

In a newer kitchen the lights will probably be on their own circuit, but in an older home they may share a circuit with the receptacles or appliances.

Understanding Electrical Capacity

When you open the door of your service panel you may find a chart (or map) telling you which electrical users are on which circuit. If you don't have such a chart, you can learn by experience: when a circuit blows, note which receptacles, lights, and appliances are de-energized. Write those down, and note which circuit breaker covers them.

Now you can do some simple calculating. Most circuits are 120 volts and have a capacity of either 15 or 20 amps. (The circuit breaker or fuse will tell you which.) To be safe, however, codes require that a 15-amp circuit should pull only 12 amps, and a 20-amp circuit should pull only 16 amps. Because many appliances are rated by watts rather than amps, let's translate this into watts: A 15-amp circuit should pull no more than 1,440 watts, and a 20-amp circuit should pull no more than 1,920 watts. (In case you're interested, the formula is: watts ÷ volts = amps.)

With this basic knowledge, you can look at all the electrical users—lights, hardwired appliances, and appliances that plug in and are often used—and add up either their amps or wattages to find whether a circuit is overloaded or not. Look at the information plates on the appliances and the wattage ratings of the lightbulbs, and do some simple addition to find out.

For instance, a 15-amp circuit will be overloaded if it supplies a 1,200-watt toaster plus a 900-watt microwave (for a total of 2,100 watts) at the same time.

If you want to install, say, a new 1,000-watt hot-water dispenser, either make sure it is on a circuit that does not use much more electricity or have an electrician install a new circuit for it.

Note that a refrigerator should be on its own dedicated circuit because if it overloads, food could spoil. And 220-volt appliances like electric cooktops and ovens are always on their own circuits.

A kitchen needs circuits that safely supply power for lights, receptacles (which often supply small appliances), and appliances like a dishwasher and a waste-disposal unit.

Dishwasher

Newer dishwashers are available with some attractive features, such as adjustable racks and loading aids that allow you to stack up to one-third more dishes and glasses; heating elements that raise water temperature higher than your hottest tap water; and control buttons placed on top of the door, so they are hidden when the door is closed. Be sure to buy a model with two spray arms; it will clean glasses in the upper rack much better than a model with only one arm.

Replacing a dishwasher is easier than you may think. There are typically three lines to disconnect (electric, water supply, and drain) and two screws holding the dishwasher in place.

If you have no existing dishwasher, you can install a new one in the space occupied by a 24-inch base cabinet. You will need to run an electrical line (on its own circuit), a flexible water supply line connected to a stop valve (usually, under the sink), and a drain hose from the sink's plumbing. Hire a professional electrician or plumber for these tasks if you are not sure about your abilities.

Replacing a Dishwasher

- **Dishwasher, which typically comes with a drain hose, water**

1 Shut off the stop valve (probably under the sink) that supplies water to the dishwasher. Shut off the power at the service panel. Remove screws, and pull out the access panel at the bottom of the unit. Disconnect the water supply line; place a bowl under it to catch water that will dribble out (inset). Remove the electrical box's cover; disconnect the wires; and remove the cable.

4 If the water supply is flexible copper tubing, work carefully and make only slow bends to avoid kinking the tubing. Slide on a nut and ferrule; slip the tubing's end into the inlet; slide the ferrule and nut tight against the inlet; and tighten the nut. If there is a flexible metal-braided supply line, simply tighten its nut onto the inlet.

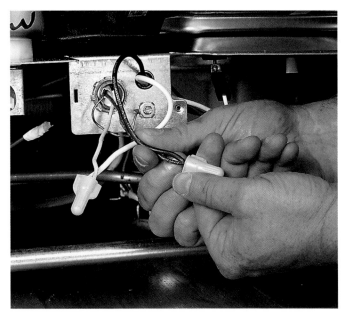

5 To make the electrical connection, remove the cover plate, which is usually held with one screw. Thread the cable's wires through the hole, and clamp the cable at the back of the box. Connect like-colored dishwasher leads with the wires; then cap them using wire connectors. Connect the ground wire to the grounding screw. Replace the cover plate.

supply line, and hose clamps • Bucket • Adjustable wrench and groove-joint pliers • Screwdriver • Flashlight

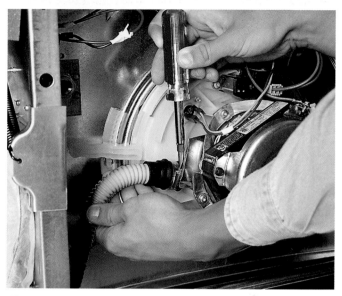

2 Loosen the screw on the clamp that holds the drain hose, and pull the hose off; have a bowl handy to catch dribbling water. Remove the screws holding the unit in place; they may be driven up into the underside of the countertop or sideways into the cabinets on either side. Slide the dishwasher out, taking care not to snag any of the lines.

3 Slide the new dishwasher partway into the opening, taking care to position the plumbing and electrical lines so you can reach them. Attach the drain hose. In some models the inlet is accessible from the front bottom, behind the access panel; on other models it is near the rear. Use the hose clamp or the grip ring that's supplied. Loosen and slide the clamp over; slip on the hose; and slide and retighten the clamp.

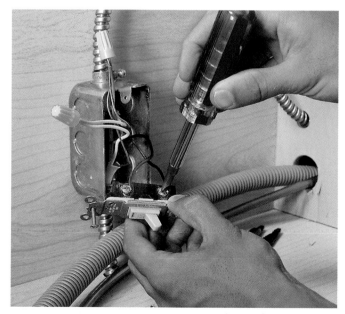

6 Some codes require that a dishwasher be controlled by a switch rather than direction connection to the service panel. For the former, install a switch box in the cabinet next to the dishwasher. Run cable from the panel box to the switch box; run cable from the appliance to the switch box. Join like-color white and ground wires as shown. Attach the black wires to the switch.

7 Slowly push the dishwasher into the cabinet opening. Use a wrench to turn the leveling legs so the front of the machine is plumb and aligned with the front of the cabinets. You may need to pull the machine out and adjust the legs at the back. Drive two screws up through the fastening brackets and into the underside of the countertop or (if you have a granite top) through the sides of the machine and into the cabinets.

Range Hood

Some homes do not have a range hood, and others have a hood that is not vented to the outside. Today's serious cooks prefer a ducted range hood to carry away smoke, heat, and odors. (Only a very strong commercial unit will suck out spattering grease.) Ductwork can travel in a number of directions. Choose the shortest and easiest route. If your cooktop is on an interior wall in a one-story building, you may choose to go through the roof. If you do not already have electrical cable running to the hood location, have an electrician install it.

If you will replace a range hood that is already ducted to the outside, the job is pretty simple: Make the electrical connections; then attach the existing ductwork to the new unit (you may need to buy an adapter duct piece).

This high-end range hood has a powerful, quiet motor and four lights to really light up all of your cooking pots.

Ducting Options

If you run the ducting through a soffit, install a transition elbow fitting to connect the round duct to the square grill ❶. If the duct passes through the roof, install a weatherproof duct cap: cut an opening in the roof so the duct can protrude. Then cut shingles as needed and slide the cap over the duct. The cap's flange should rest under the shingles at its top half and over shingles at its bottom half. Seal with plastic roof cement ❷.

Installing a Range Hood

• Range hood • Electrical cable and supplies • Jigsaw and drill • Aviator shears (tin snips) • Ductwork sized to fit the unit
• Sheet metal screws and professional-quality duct tape

1 Shut off power to the electrical circuit. (See page 171.) Cut the wall or the cabinet as needed to run ductwork out the wall or through the roof. Here we show a common method, running ducting through a hole in the cabinet above. Cut a hole in the outside wall or roof as well.

2 Remove the electrical cover from the hood. Pull the power cable out; thread its wires though the hood; and secure the cable with a cable clamp. Splice like-colored wires and range leads together, and screw on wire connectors (inset). Replace the cover. Remove a ducting knockout, and install the duct adapter onto the hood. Working with a helper, thread the cable back into the wall as you raise the range hood into position up against the underside of a cabinet. Drive screws into the cabinet above and into adjacent cabinets to secure it.

3 Run ductwork through the wall or roof. Cut the pieces with aviation shears; join them together; and drive three self-tapping sheet-metal screws into each joint. Two 45-deg. adjustable elbows will usually do the job. Cover the joints with duct tape.

4 If the duct comes out the side of the house, cut and install it so it protrudes a little; then slip on a duct cap. Seal around its perimeter with caulking.

Gas Range

A new range can quickly change the appearance and feel of a kitchen, not to mention improving your cooking options. Removing and replacing one is usually a fairly simple task. However, be sure to buy a new corrugated stainless-steel tubing (CSST) line to connect the range to the house's gas-line shutoff valve. Depending on the design and manufacturer of your range and shutoff valve, this line may have a ½-inch fitting on each end or a ½-inch fitting on one end and a ¾-inch fitting on the other. This line may be plain stainless steel, or it may be yellow coated. Do not reuse an old brass flexible line; these fittings are considered unsafe. And if the CSST does not fit onto your shutoff valve, call in a plumber to see whether you need a new valve or not.

Replacing a Gas Range

• Gas range • Flexible CSST gas line • Adjustable wrenches, or wrench and groove-joint pliers • Brush and soapy water

1 To be safe, shut off the house's main gas shutoff, located in a basement, crawlspace, or outside. Lift the old range's front legs onto a drop cloth, and carefully slide it away to reveal the gas shutoff valve. Turn off the valve, and use a wrench to loosen and remove the flexible line. Remove the old stove, and buy a new flexible gas line long enough to attach to the valve with the range a couple of feet away from the wall. You or your spouse may want to take this opportunity to clean the floor under the range

2 Tighten the new flexible line to the range and to the shutoff valve. Use two wrenches or pliers, one to hold the valve still while you tighten with the other one. Turn on the gas. Check for leaks by spreading soapy water on the joints. If you see bubbles, you have a leak. (You may not smell a slow but very dangerous leak.) If tightening the nut does not solve the problem, call in a plumber.

3 Once you are sure there are no leaks, plug the electrical cord into the wall. Push the range against the wall, taking care not to scratch the floor or kink the flexible gas line. Level the range by adjusting the feet using pliers. You may need to pull out the range and adjust the rear feet as well.

Cooktop

Replacing a cooktop is a surprisingly easy job, as long as it fits in the same hole as the existing one. Here we show installing an electric unit. A gas cooktop installs in much the same way, but you connect its flexible line to a gas shutoff valve and test it, as you would for a range (previous page). If you want to install a cooktop where there is no existing one, call in an electrician or plumber to supply approved electrical or gas hookups. An electric cooktop runs to a dedicated 220-volt circuit breaker in the service panel. There is usually an electrical junction box inside the cabinet, below the cooktop.

Be Up to Code

TIP

Check with your local building department before installing a new electric cooktop. The latest National Electric Code states that if a circuit is new, the appliance's cable must have a separate ground wire, and it should be wired hot to hot, neutral to neutral, and ground to ground.

Replacing a Cooktop

• Cooktop • Armored cable • Materials for an electrical connection or gas line with shutoff • Drill and saber saw

1 At your electrical service panel, shut off the cooktop's 220-volt breaker. To remove the old cooktop, unscrew its mounting clips; open the electrical box; and disconnect the wires. If new cooktop does not fit into the existing hole, use the unit's template to trace a cut line, and cut using a saber saw. Test-fit the cooktop by lowering it into the opening.

2 Check to be sure that the cooktop's cable will reach the junction box. Apply silicone caulk to the bottom of the rim, and lower the cooktop into the hole. From inside the cabinet, attach the mounting clips by driving short screws.

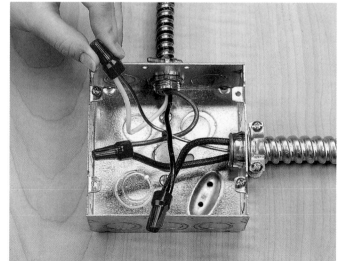

3 Verify that power is off in the junction box. Bring the new cable from the appliance into the box, and tighten the cable clamps. Use wire connectors to splice the red wires, then the black wires. Join the white and ground wires.

Kitchen Connections

A kitchen is not an office or a living room, but you may want to include a television, music source, or computer with internet access. You could simply put any of these things on a countertop or table, but there are products that take them up off of the countertop to restore counter space and make them easier to get access to.

Internet Access

A Kindle or other electronic book device can consolidate all of your favorite cookbooks in a compact, portable case. It frees up shelf space in the kitchen. To protect the device from inevitable spills and spatters, you can keep the device in a clear plastic protector, the sort of thing you'd find at an office store. Or use a cookbook stand or an under-counter cookbook holder to make it easier to read. Book readers usually don't offer internet access, or if they do, it may be a slow connection and difficult to read.

Netbooks are increasingly popping up on kitchen counters or shelves. A thin, lightweight computer with a screen size that's 12 inches or smaller, a netbook brings Wifi access to your kitchen. A netbook lets you check messages or maintain an instant message dialogue, download recipes, and listen to music, all while you work in the kitchen. If you keep your charger in the kitchen, too, your battery will be ready to go the next morning.

An iPad has all the same advantages of a netbook, plus it's more flexible for positioning. Some people keep one on a wall in a frame in a central place in the kitchen. Of course, you can also use a laptop computer, but it will have to rest on a countertop or table.

Music

If your kitchen is wired into a multi-room audio system, you need only mount speakers in the kitchen, perhaps near the ceiling where they're out of the way. But if you don't yet have that, a countertop dock for an iPod or iPad with speakers and a charger will bring a nice selection of music into the kitchen.

Television

Today's TVs made for kitchens have built-in tuners, which makes it easier to connect a secondary TV to your home's cable, satellite, etc. Most people will need a little technical assistance to get the connections working, but this is easier to accomplish than it used to be.

Probably the most common place for a kitchen TV is on the counter in a back corner that would otherwise be dead space. But if you'd like to add a flat-panel TV to your kitchen, you'll want to mount it. That can be tricky because most kitchens have limited wall space. One solution is a mount with a long arm that can be swiveled—which makes it possible to put the TV in a space next to the kitchen and turn it toward the area of the kitchen where you're working—or an under-cabinet mount.

A wall-mounted bracket, screwed into a wall stud, is positioned behind the TV or tablet, so the screen seems to float. With most brackets, the screen can be pulled out or swiveled for a good view from anywhere in the room.

Hand-Held Devices

If you have a hand-held device with internet access (iPod or iPhone, for example), it may be handy to keep the charger in the kitchen. Many chargers also have speakers for a stereo effect and a stand that makes it easy to read a recipe. Depending on the capabilities of your device, you may have access to a host of helpful kitchen apps, each costing only a few dollars—an app to help find a recipe based on the ingredients you have on hand or the ingredients you like to cook with, for instance, or an app to help you organize your shopping lists. You may also be able to listen to podcasts of cooking shows or even watch cooking shows.

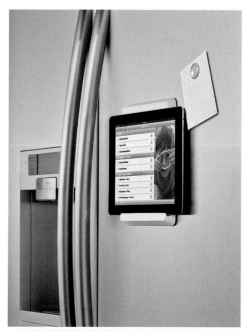

A desktop charging station, above left, can organize laptops and tablets as well as phones.

A large ceiling-mounted TV, top right, can be easily viewed from all parts of the kitchen.

A tablet holder like the one at far left may be mounted with adhesive or magnets.

This mounting bracket for a tablet, left, can quickly attach to almost any table and allows you to swivel the tablet for the best viewing angle.

8

Flooring

This chapter will help you choose your finish flooring and will show all of the steps needed to install it. Those steps include the preparation of the subfloor, which is just as important as the flooring itself. Subfloor requirements depend on the type of flooring you already have, the finish material you choose, and the flooring height you want to achieve. In some cases you may be able to simply install new flooring over the flooring you already have, but it's more likely that you will need to install some sort of subflooring. And you may need to tear out existing flooring before you begin.

Choosing Flooring

Kitchen flooring options are even more varied than countertop and backsplash options. And most products today are not only good looking but also durable and easy to clean. Once you subtract the square footage taken up by cabinets, a kitchen floor is usually not very large, so you may consider more-expensive materials than you would use in a living or dining room.

Colors

To help choose colors that blend well with your cabinets and countertops, take a cabinet door and a leftover countertop scrap—or a couple of good photos with accurate colors—with you when you shop for flooring. Flooring of a similar color recedes visually, while sharply contrasting color adds interest.

Natural hardwood strip flooring and stone (or ceramic stone-look) tiles are safe choices because they harmonize with almost everything. If you prefer more-colorful ceramic or vinyl tiles, be careful to avoid a clash.

Resilient or Hard?

Wood, vinyl, and laminate flooring are resilient, meaning that they provide underfoot "give," which some people find has a welcome cushioning effect, especially in a surface where they do plenty of standing. Resilient flooring has another plus: a dropped glass or plate has a better chance of survival than if it were dropped on a harder surface.

Other people prefer the solid look and feel, as well as the warm natural tones, of ceramic or stone tile. They may argue that if your feet get tired, you should just wear more-comfortable shoes. And hard tiles are generally more durable and washable than resilient products.

Resilient flooring can be installed over a subfloor that has a bit of give. Ceramic or stone tiles must rest on a rock-solid substrate, or they will crack. That may mean you will have to beef up your subfloor, often by installing ½-inch concrete backer board. Doing so may raise the floor ½ inch or more above the living room or other adjacent floor, which can create a tripping hazard or at least an inconvenience. If that is the case, you may choose to go with an easy-to-install resilient flooring instead.

Wood Flooring

Modern polyurethane coatings are easy to apply and effectively resist water and scratches, making wood flooring a

practical option for a kitchen. Still, wood flooring does call for more maintenance—perhaps even yearly recoating—than ceramic or stone tile.

Wood flooring is often called "strip" flooring, because it comes in long, narrow boards that join together via tongues and grooves along their edges. Solid strip flooring is simply made of wood that is ¾ inch thick. Once installed, it will need to be sanded smooth, then stained and finished—processes that take several days. "Engineered" strip flooring can be walked on as soon as it is installed. It is made of plywood, with a top veneer of hardwood that may be ¼ inch thick, depending on the manufacturer. It often has small chamfers all along where the boards meet, and so is slightly more difficult to clean when installed than a sanded solid-wood floor. It comes with a factory-applied hard finish, which you may need to restore every few years with coats of polyurethane.

Blond-colored maple is the classic kitchen flooring material. But you can also choose South American hardwoods. Pine and other softwoods have a distressed, cottagey look, but they dent easily and are difficult to keep clean. Oak flooring that is simply coated with a clear finish like polyurethane may look out of place in a kitchen, but if you apply a dark stain first, it can be quite fetching.

Cork flooring is available in wide float-ing planks or in 12- or 24-in. squares. Some flooring is available as "mosaic" cork tiles, left, with patterns that can be arranged as you choose.

Laminate flooring, above, comes in a wide variety of colors, textures, and sheens.

Stone-look tiles that are actually made of glazed porcelain, right, give you a floor that is stronger than a stone-tile floor and extremely easy to keep clean.

Vinyl Tile

Vinyl tiles have a printed pattern, a factory-applied finish, and often a cushioned backing. Vinyl composition tile, also called commercial tile, needs to be coated with acrylic or other finish. Installing tiles is a popular do-it-yourself project.

Laminate

This flooring is made of a thin plastic laminate—harder than a laminate countertop surface—bonded to a fiberboard core. The laminate is often printed to look like natural wood, but patterns are also available. The flooring is easy to keep clean and effectively resists most attempts to scratch it. If a scratch does occur, however, it will be impossible to fix.

Ceramic Tile

A ceramic floor can be easy to maintain, as long as it is installed with the right grout and grout sealants. Unglazed tiles, such as quarry tiles, are slip resistant, but some types will stain unless you coat them with finish. Most glazed tiles are virtually impervious to staining. Porcelain tiles, whether shiny or matte, are impervious to staining and very strong, even though they are thinner than most other ceramics. Mexican Saltillo tiles are soft, but their gentle beauty makes the extra maintenance well worth it. Installing a solid subfloor and ceramic tile is an ambitious project, but many homeowners have accomplished it.

Stone Tile

Stone tiles are simply cut out of the earth, and so each tile has its own unique pattern and color. Most of these tiles are as easy to install as ceramic, but some are irregular in shape, providing you with an extra challenge when laying them. The most common stone tile is slate, but honed marble and other natural stones are also available. Many of these tiles soak up stains like a sponge, so they need to be covered with a flooring sealer, and perhaps an acrylic or polyurethane finish over that.

Other Materials

- Cork is a natural and renewable material, and it provides a nice springiness underfoot. It is sometimes available as separate tiles that must be installed using special cork adhesive, but more often it is sold as the top layer of laminated strips.

- True linoleum (not sheet vinyl) is made of resins, stone chips, fibers, and other natural ingredients. Each sheet has one-of-a-kind patterns of swirls and splotches. An expert linoleum installer can make custom patterns by inlaying sections of various colored sheets.

- Bamboo flooring installs just like strip wood but is made from a plant that is actually a grass. Choose bamboo carefully; some less-expensive types develop pits and divots, while better products wear like iron.

These vinyl tiles, left, have a sophisticated appearance but are very inexpensive and easy to install. As a bonus, they will not crack when laid on a subfloor that is a less than solid.

Ceramic tiles with the look of travertine, top left, make for a no-fuss floor with a clean and orderly feel.

Vinyl tiles that have variegated colors, a raised pattern, and edges that match up to mimic the look of grout joints, above, closely imitate the look of a stone or ceramic tile floor but are much less expensive and do not require a super-strong subsurface.

Painting a Kitchen Floor

The quickest, cheapest, and easiest way to transform a dingy wood floor is to paint it. A painted floor can be surprisingly durable if you do it right. And if it does chip or dull, you can always paint over it again. Use durable paint, such as 100-percent acrylic. But the real hardness comes from applying several coats of polyurethane. These two pages show painting a solid color; the following four pages show making a checkerboard pattern.

An older hardwood floor with visible gaps between some of the boards can be easily painted to create a cottage effect. The putty color shown here is one of many choices that will deemphasize dust and debris, and it harmonizes well with the simple rosy-hued rug.

Getting It Really Dry

Water-based paints and finishes dry to the touch quickly but take a long time to really harden. It's important to get that paint as hard as possible before walking on it. Wait an hour or so for the paint to surface-dry; then direct a fan at it. You don't need a blast of wind; a gentle breeze will greatly speed up drying. Wait at least a day, preferably two or three, before using the floor.

TIP

How to Paint a Kitchen Floor

• Pole sander with 80-grit sandpaper • Cleaning tool and detergent • Paint • Paintbrush, pole, and duct tape • Polyurethane finish

1 Use a pole sander to roughen up the entire floor. If you don't do this, the paint may peel in time, especially if the floor has a glossy finish. If you encounter any high spots, scrape them down so that the floor is fairly smooth.

2 Clean away any oils and gunky spots. Apply TSP (trisodium phosphate) or another heavy-duty cleaner; then rinse and allow to dry.

3 Paint the edges with a brush. Attaching a brush to a pole with some duct tape creates a tool that allows you to do this while standing. Go ahead and slop the paint onto a wall or cabinet bottom if you will cover it later with base trimwork or base cove.

4 Most older floors have gaps between the strips. It's usually not a good idea to try to fill in these gaps; it's really hard to fill them in, and the filler can look unnatural. Instead, learn to enjoy the rustic cottage ambiance. Allow the paint to dry for a day or more; apply another coat if needed; and cover it with polyurethane finish.

Painting a Floor Pattern

Creating a pattern will add hours to the time you spend painting a floor, but the result can be playful and inviting. In addition to the checkerboard pattern shown here, you can use much the same methods to create a border that runs around the kitchen, perhaps parallel with the cabinets, or a distinctive pattern in the middle of the floor.

Whichever pattern you choose, start by painting the base color, and give it a day or more to dry. On graph paper, make a scale drawing of your kitchen floor with the pattern you will create. Use colored pencils to mimic the paint colors you will use. Transfer the drawing to the floor, using a straightedge and pencil or a chalk line. Then apply painter's tape along the lines to mask off the areas you do not want to paint. Apply the second color of paint, and remove the tape. Allow the paint to dry fully, and apply a coat of polyurethane.

Layout Tips

TIP

When you make your pattern drawing, plan the layout to avoid small partial squares (or other design elements) along a wall or row of cabinets. Start by placing full-size squares at the most visible wall. If that results in narrow slivers along the opposite wall, you may choose to adjust the size of the squares. (On most floors, squares ranging from 9 to 14 inches will look fine.) Or split the difference and have half-size squares along each wall.

To draw a diagonal checkerboard layout on the floor, start by snapping two diagonal lines—perpendicular to each other—near the center of the floor; then measure out from those lines to make layout marks in each direction.

The more-complicated pattern here will call for careful planning and marking of each square to keep the colors straight.

How to Paint a Floor Pattern

• Measuring tape, pencil, and chalk-line box • Painter's tape (which works better than masking tape) • Scissors • Putty knife
• Floor paint • Brush or small roller • Polyurethane finish

1 Mark for the layout lines. Following your plan, measure and mark the floor for evenly spaced layout lines in both directions. Make marks along all four walls.

2 Working with a helper, snap chalk lines between the layout marks. Check that the chalk-line box has plenty of blue chalk. (Red and other colors may permanently stain.) Pull the line out carefully, so it doesn't touch the floor. Pull taut, and place the line over the layout marks. Lift the line up, and let go to create a perfectly straight line.

3 Reel in the line, and repeat until all of the lines are made. Stand back, and inspect to make sure you didn't go off track. Place an X mark made of painter's tape in every other square, where you will not paint the new color.

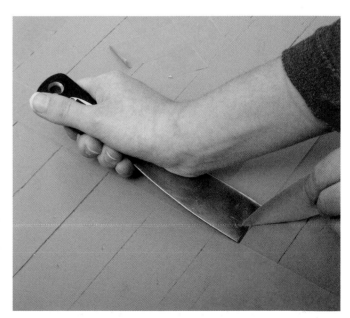

4 Apply tape to outline the squares that will get painted with the new color. Have a helper supply you with many strips of tape that are a couple of inches longer than you need. (Cut them with scissors rather than ripping them.) Apply the tape; then use a sharp putty knife to cut the end exactly at the end of the square.

Continued on next page

How to Paint a Floor Pattern, cont'd.

5 After laying down the tape, run the putty knife along the edge that abuts where the new color will be to firmly press it into place. If the tape is not tightly sealed, paint can seep under it

6 Continue applying tape. Always apply the tape onto the side of the line that faces an X mark. Every once in a while, stand back and examine your work; it's easy to make mistakes and put the tape on the wrong side of the line.

7 Apply the new paint inside the squares that do not have Xs. A small roller works well for this. If you use a brush instead, brush away from the tape rather than toward it to lessen the chance of slipping paint under the tape.

8 Allow the paint to dry for at least an hour; then pull up the tape. Wear clean clothes, and have clean hands as you do this to avoid smudging the paint, which will still not be completely dry. Direct a fan onto the floor, and wait a day or more; then apply polyurethane finish, and allow it to dry in the same way.

Preparing and Planning a Subfloor

The framing and sheathing that lie beneath finished flooring material—the subfloor—are as important as the flooring itself. Different types of flooring have different subflooring requirements, but all subfloors should be at least close to level and at least fairly strong. If you suspect major structural problems with your subfloor or perhaps the presence of termites or other wood-eating critters, call in a professional carpenter or exterminator.

The Right Height and Transitions

As you plan your subflooring and flooring, bear in mind the finished height of the new floor. If the kitchen floor is ½ inch or more higher than an adjacent floor, such as a living room or dining room, then you will have what many people consider an awkward step up every time you enter the kitchen.

Step-ups of less than ½ inch can be gracefully handled using transition strips (or thresholds). A good variety of strips can be found to fit many situations, including a transition from wood or ceramic to a carpeted floor. Metal strips that overlay the joint are are the easiest to cut and install, but they are unattractive and create a bump in the floor. Strips that do not overlay the flooring (like the ones shown at right) require precise cutting of the flooring, but they are far better looking and make for a smoother transition.

Sometimes you can install finish flooring—or underlayment, then the flooring—directly onto the existing floor. Often, however, that will raise the floor too high, and you will have to remove the old flooring. Depending

on the flooring, you may need to use a pry bar and hammer or a flooring scraper. In some cases it helps to cut

out sections, using a circular saw with its blade set to cut only through the portion that you want to remove.

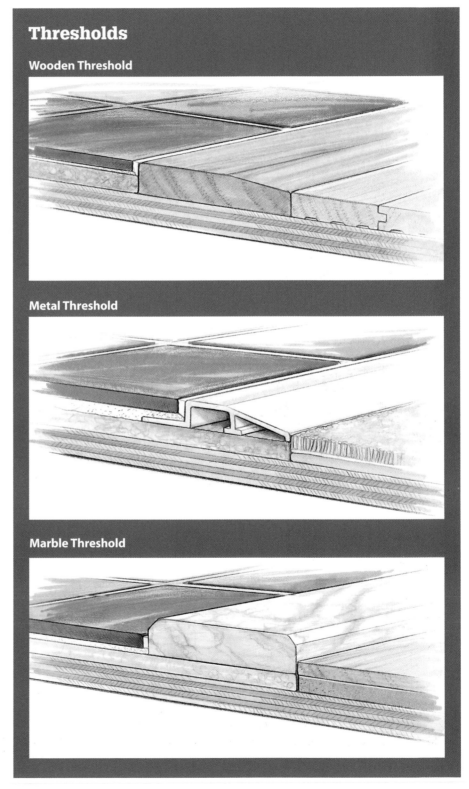

Thresholds

Wooden Threshold

Metal Threshold

Marble Threshold

Strengthening a Floor

If a floor feels bouncy, squeaks, or has low spots, you may be able to strengthen it. First try pulling out any loose nails; then drive screws through the subflooring and into joists below ❶. Drive screws every 10 inches in the middle of a plywood sheet and every 6 inches around the perimeter.

If the ceiling below is unfinished, you can check the joists. Hold a 4-foot level on the bottom of the joists to see whether any of them sag ❷. If a joist sags more than ½ inch, reinforce it.

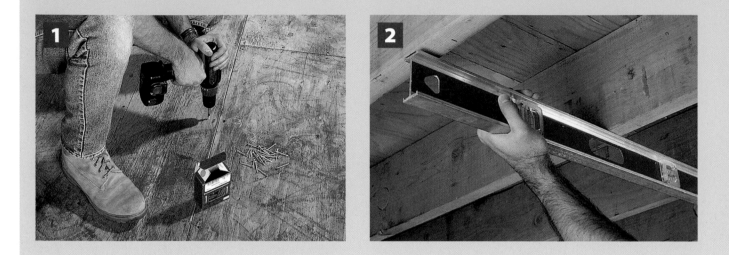

Installing Plywood Underlayment

• Plywood • Circular saw and scrap lumber • Measuring tape, pencil, and chalk-line box • Drill-driver and screws

1 Whether you will install resilient or hard flooring, a plywood underlayment is often called for. (To install thin plywood underlayment for vinyl tile or sheets, see pages 223-24.) Choose plywood of a thickness that will cause the flooring to match the height of adjacent floors. Install the sheets with staggered joints.

2 Cut the plywood on sawhorses or on scrap boards. Mark the length on both edges, and snap a chalk line between the two marks. Set a circular saw's blade depth so that it doesn't hit the floor, and cut the sheets.

To strengthen a sagging joist, cut a "sister" piece out of the same 2-by lumber as the joist, 6 feet or longer. Prop the joist by wedging a 4×4 under it or by using a flooring jack. Attach the sister to the joist with a grid of 2½-inch screws ❸.

3 Note the locations of joists, and write down their distances from the wall so you can drive screws into them later. Place the sheets with a ⅛-in. gap at walls or cabinets to allow for expansion. Lay the sheets so that the joints will be staggered by at least 3 in. Drive screws that are long enough to penetrate at least 1½ in. into the joists below. Drive screws every 6 in. along the perimeter of the sheets and every 10 in. in the middle.

Checking for Level

To see whether a floor is level or not, place a 4 foot level on a long, straight 2×4. If the floor is more than ½ inch out of level in a 10 foot span, it will be noticeable where the wall or cabinets meet the floor. Set some pieces of the finished floor in place to see whether you can live with the discrepancy or not. If not, pull up the sheathing, and install shims on top of joists to bring the flooring up to level.

Checking for Square

Many kitchen floors are out of square, especially in older homes. An out-of-square condition can wreak havoc on a flooring layout, causing you to install boards or tiles that are misaligned with cabinets or walls. Check your corners for square before you lay out the floor. Lay a sheet of plywood with two factory edges against the corner. Or use the 3-4-5 method: measure from the corner along one wall to the 3-foot point, and mark the floor. Mark on the other wall at 4 feet. If the diagonal distance between the two marks is 5 feet, the room is square. If the corner is out of square, make your layout lines correspond with a square line rather than the wall.

Installing Hardwood Strip Flooring

Laying and finishing solid hardwood flooring is a challenging and time-consuming task. Installing engineered flooring is a far quicker and simpler procedure, so you may want to choose it instead. But solid hardwood, once sanded and finished, is harder and more resistant to dents; it is perfectly smooth; and it can be resanded and refinished several times, making it worth the extra trouble in the long run.

Fastening the Flooring

Check the existing floor for level, strength, and squareness as shown on pages 205–7. To get the floor at the correct height, you may need to remove one or more layers of the existing floor and subfloor.

A natural hardwood floor that is sanded and stained may be a bit pricy and time-consuming to install, but the result is a smooth, graceful, and naturally elegant surface that no other material can quite match.

Fastening the Floor

- Basic carpentry tools • 15-lb. roofing hand-driven flooring stapler or nailer

1 Remove moldings at the bottom of walls and cabinets. If there is both wide base molding and smaller base shoe, you may choose to remove only the shoe. If you want to reuse moldings, carefully pull nails out from the back, using groove-joint pliers, and label them by location.

5 Once you are far enough away from the wall, use a tongue-and-groove flooring nailer or stapler. A pneumatic stapler is easiest to use, but you can also use a hand-driven flooring nailer. Drive fasteners every 8 in. or so.

felt (tar paper) • Hardwood flooring (get an extra 10% for waste) • Backsaw • Drill • Power miter saw and saber saw • Pneumatic or

2 Use a piece of scrap flooring to undercut doorway casing boards so that the flooring can slip under it. Lay 15-lb. roofing felt across the entire floor, taking care not to crease it, and staple it in place.

3 The first line of boards should be positioned tongue-out, and ³/₈ in. or so away from the wall to allow for expansion. Place spacers against the wall; then snap a chalk line for the first board. Face-nail the first boards with a power nailer, or drill pilot holes and hand-drive finish nails. Set the nails deep into the flooring.

4 Lay out several rows of boards. See that all adjacent—and one-away-from-adjacent—joints are staggered by at least 1½ in. If boards vary in color, arrange them in a pleasing pattern.

Keep Things Tight

TIP

Tap each board gently with the rubber side of the nailer's mallet to snug it against the previous board. If a board is warped and won't tap over, drive a chisel into the subfloor next to it, and pry it over. If that doesn't work, discard the board, and use a straighter one.

6 When you reach the end of a row, hold the board with the tongue facing backwards against a spacer, and mark for cutting. Cut with a power miter saw or circular saw.

7 When you reach the last boards you will again need to face-nail the boards. If needed, use a pry bar and a spacer to pull the board tight before driving the fastener.

Refinishing (or Finishing) a Floor

• Broom • Floor sander and sandpaper • Edge sander • Hand scraper • Shop vac, damp cloth • Lamb's wool applicator, polyurethane

Engineered hardwood flooring like this does not need to be sanded and stained. It is, however, a good idea to apply two coats of polyurethane to seal the joints.

Sanding

Once laid, a hardwood floor must be sanded to create a monolithic, smooth surface. You may want to hire professionals to do this because it's easy to create pits or waves in the floor if you handle the machines incorrectly. If you want to do it yourself, rent a drum sander, a sanding edger, and a buffer. A 220-volt drum sander works more efficiently, but a 120-volt model will get the job done. Sanding will create a great deal of fine, insidious dust, so seal off doorways and heat registers with plastic sheeting and duct tape. Wear a respirator to protect your lungs from dust and fumes.

3 Use a hand scraper to remove existing finish (if any) from the corners where an edger cannot reach. The scraper is also a good tool for removing any scratches left from the edge sander.

4 Use a shop-vac, then a very slightly damp cloth, to remove all dust from the floor. If desired, apply stain, and allow to dry. Use a lamb's wool applicator to apply polyurethane finish. Apply in smooth, long strokes to avoid creating bubbles.

finish · Buffer

1 Sweep the floor, and check to be sure all face nails are driven at least ¼ in. into the flooring. Equip the sander with 40-grit sandpaper, and sand in the direction of the grain. Move slowly, but never stop even for a second while the drum is turning, or you could create a dip. Repeat the process with 60-grit, then 80-grit paper. If you will apply a dark stain, also use 100-grit paper.

2 Use an edge sander to remove finish close to the walls. Again, sand with a rough-grit paper; then use progressively finer papers until all the circular sand marks are invisible.

5 Allow the first coat of finish to dry; then buff with a rotary buffer with a fine steel-wool pad attached. Keep the buffer moving at all times, and move in the direction of the strips.

6 Vacuum away all dust and steel-wool particles; then clean with a slightly damp cloth. Apply one or two more coats of polyurethane, followed by buffing and vacuuming.

Preparing for Ceramic- or Stone-Tile Flooring

Here the number-one consideration is subfloor strength; if the floor flexes even a little bit, the grout or even the tiles may crack. If you feel the floor flex when an adult jumps on it, the floor is probably not strong enough. Generally, the subfloor is strong enough if the framing is strong, with joists every 16 inches, and is covered by a layer of ¾-inch plywood topped with ½-inch concrete backer board. See pages 206–7 for installing plywood underlayment and for ways to firm up a subfloor. If you are unsure about your subfloor strength, consult with a professional tile setter.

Installing Backer Board

Unless you have a concrete floor, it's almost always a good idea to install concrete or fiber-cement backer board, to really firm up the floor. Half-inch backer board is the most common because of its strength, but even ¼-inch backer board will also add some firmness. Cut backer board much as you would drywall, by scoring one side, snapping, and slicing through the other side. However, backer board is harder to cut; you need to cut through its embedded fiber mesh.

A sumptuous limestone or honed marble floor feels smooth but requires a subsur-face that is rock-solid to keep the tiles from cracking.

Installing Backer Board

• Backer board • Backer-board scoring tool or utility knife • Thinset mortar • Trowel with a flat side • Backer-board screws • Fiberglass mesh

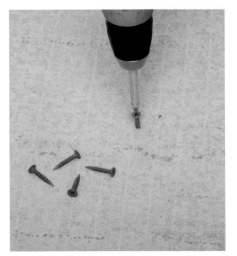

1 Mark the panel for the cut. Score the line using a utility knife or backer-board scoring tool. It's easiest to score the first line with the board lying on the floor. Break the panel against your knee or over a piece of scrap placed on the floor.

2 Place the panel on edge, and slice through the fiberglass mesh on the back. Bend the panel back to complete the cut.

3 Trowel mortar onto the floor, and set the panels in the mortar. Drive backer-board screws (not drywall screws, which are difficult to embed) in an 8-in. grid.

Laying Out for Tiles

After checking the room for square (page 207), plan the layout so that no row of narrow-cut tiles appears in a conspicuous place, such as at a doorway or along cabinets. When planning the layout, take into account the size of the tiles and the width of the grout lines. If, for instance, you have 8-inch tiles with ¼-inch grout lines, think of each tile as 8¼ inches.

It's best to start your calculations by drawing perpendicular centerlines on the floor. Check with a sheet of plywood or a framing square to be sure they are perpendicular. Dry-lay tiles, with the plastic spacers, from the centerlines and out to the walls or cabinets in several places. If you find that you end up with a narrow row at one or both sides, adjust the centerline so that you end up with rows of half-size or wider tiles.

If you will lay tiles diagonally, start with the same two centerlines; then add two lines at 45 degrees to them. From the center point, measure out an equal distance along any two of the lines, and drive a nail at these two points, marked A and B on the drawing below. Hook the ends of a measuring tape to each of the nails, and hold a pencil against the tape at a distance equal to that between the nails and center point. Use the tape and pencil as a compass to scribe two arcs on the floor that will intersect at point C. Snap a chalk line between the center point and point C; then do the same thing on the other side of the room.

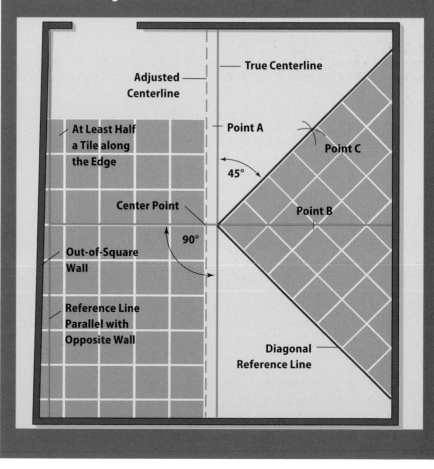

4 Trowel mortar onto the floor, and set the sheet in the mortar. Apply fiberglass mesh tape to the joints, and trowel mortar over the joints.

Ceramic-Tile Flooring

Once you have removed baseboards and other obstructions and firmed up the floor (pages 206–7), and the floor is firmed up with backer board (as shown on pages 212–13) or with another layer of plywood (as shown on these pages), you are ready to tile. Depending on the type of tile you have, you may need a wet-cutting tile saw for all cuts, or you may be able to make most cuts using a snap cutter. Notches and cutouts are easiest to make with a wet saw, but if you have only a few, you can use a grinder equipped with a masonry blade.

Using a Laser Level TIP

An inexpensive battery-powered laser level emits an easy-to-see light beam in a perfectly straight line. Set one up so that it follows your layout line on the floor, and you won't have to hold back adhesive to keep from covering the line, as you would if you were using chalk lines only.

Glossy brown 16-in.-sq. floor tiles with narrow grout joints make for a nearly seamless floor.

Installing Ceramic-Tile Flooring

• Ceramic tiles • Thinset mortar or tile adhesive • Tile cutters • Square-notched trowel • Plastic spacers • Sanded grout
• Grout float and sponge • Grout sealer

1 Double-check your layout by setting out several rows of tiles along the chalk lines to make sure you will not have awkward-looking tile slivers at any point.

2 Mix a batch of thinset mortar, or use pre-mixed tile adhesive. Using a square-notched trowel with a notch depth that is appropriate for your tiles, spread the mortar or adhesive up to the guidelines.

3 Set the tiles into the mortar bed. Press the tiles with moderate pressure. Every once in a while, lift up a tile to make sure the adhesive is sticking to its back.

4 Use plastic spacers to maintain the grid layout. Spacers may be laid down as shown above, or they may be installed pointed upward.

5 Every few rows, place a straight board or level against the tiles to ensure straightness. This board is marked for the centers of grout lines and so doubles as a layout stick.

6 To mark for cutting tiles at a wall or cabinet, set the tile to be cut on top of the tile closest to the edge. Place another on top of it, pressed against the wall, and mark for the cut

Continued on next page

215

Installing Ceramic-Tile Flooring, cont'd.

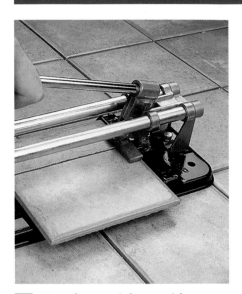

7 To make a straight cut with a snap cutter, press the tile against the cutter's front guide, so the cut will be square. Lower the cutting wheel, and either push or pull the handle (depending on the type of cutter) while pushing down to score a line. Lower the cutter's wings onto each side of the line, and push down to snap the tile.

8 To cut a notch, you can use a grinder. Or use tile nippers: nip very small pieces at a time, working gradually up to the cut line.

9 Allow the mortar at least a day to harden before walking on it. Mix a batch of grout in a bucket to the consistency of toothpaste. Allow it to slake for 10 minutes; then mix again.

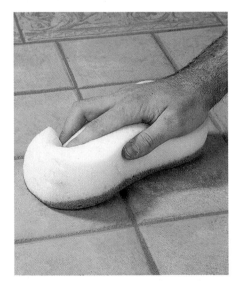

11 Fill a large bucket with water, so you can rinse the sponge many times. Using a damp sponge, wipe away excess grout. As you work, use the sponge to create grout lines of consistent depth. Continually rinse the sponge; you'll need to go over the floor several times.

12 Allow the grout to dry; then polish away the haze using cloth that is only slightly damp.

13 Wait a few days or more for the grout to fully cure; then apply grout sealer to make the grout stain resistant.

Installing Slate

If your slate tiles are consistently square and straight, install them in much the same way as ceramic tiles, using thinset mortar and plastic spacers ❶. If they are irregular in shape, use the methods shown on pages 218-21. Slate is a relatively soft stone, so you can cut it using a circular saw with a masonry blade ❷. After the grout is dry, clean and polish by sprinkling the surface with sawdust and rubbing with a burlap rag ❸. After the grout has cured, apply plenty of masonry sealer; the stone will soak it up ❹.

10 Use a grout float to push the grout into the joints. Work diagonally, so you don't dig into the joints. Then tilt the float up, and squeegee away most of the excess.

Sealing Unglazed Tiles

TIP

If you have installed quarry tiles or other unglazed tiles, seal them, and the grout, with a stone or masonry sealer. Use an applicator or a roller, pressing down to force the sealer into the grout.

Saltillo and Other Uneven Tile

Mexican Saltillo tiles have a relaxed elegance that is partly due to their irregular shapes. They are not perfectly square, and many of them are not very flat. That means that you cannot use plastic spacers, and you cannot simply set them in a bed of troweled mortar; back-buttering is the rule rather than the exception.

These tiles are easily cracked, so the subsurface must be rock solid. Remove baseboards and other obstructions, and take steps to firm up the floor with plywood and backer board. (See pages 206–7, 212–13.) Follow the general layout procedures shown on page 213 to avoid a narrow row of tiles.

Inconsistency is part of the charm of a Saltillo floor, but you should aim at installing the tiles as straight and even as possible; irregularities will occur despite your best efforts. While laying Saltillo tiles, stop every 10 minutes or so to check grout lines and spacing and eye the general layout for an appealing appearance.

Saltillo floor tiles seem to create a warm glow in a kitchen. Their earthy hues make the floor seem almost like an outside patio, yet they maintain elegance and provide a stunning background for any type of cabinet or appliance. These tiles are set at a 45-deg. angle for a diamond look.

Installing Saltillo TIle

• Backer board, screws, drill-driver • Measuring tape, pencil, framing square • Saltillo or other irregular tiles • Chalk-line box •
Thinset mortar • Bucket, mixing paddle • Notched trowel with large notches (¼ inch by ⅜ inch) • Wet-cutting tile saw • Sanded
grout • Grout float and sponge • Large towel

1 Firm up the floor, and top it with concrete or fiber-cement backer board. The floor should feel rock-solid when you jump on it.

2 Lay nine tiles in a test pattern. Decide on a pleasing grout line width (commonly ¼ in.), and place the tiles in that configuration. Measure the tile section, and add one grout-joint's width to that measurement; that's the size of your layout grids.

3 Saltillos come in various hues. To avoid having too many of one color in an area, sort them by color into three or more stacks. As you work, take tiles from each stack for each grid section, to create a "random pattern."

4 Using the measurement obtained in Step 2, use a measuring tape and pencil to draw evenly spaced marks on the floor, along all four walls or rows of cabinets. Working with a helper, snap chalk lines between the marks. Check with a framing square to be sure the grids are square and all the same size. *Continued on next page*

Installing Saltillo TIle, cont'd.

5 In a bucket, use a margin trowel or a drill with a mixing paddle to mix a batch of thinset mortar to the consistency of toothpaste. Drop a dollop of mortar into the middle of a grid square, and use a notched trowel to spread the mortar. Do not cover the layout lines.

6 Because these tiles are so porous, they may suck moisture out of the mortar, which will keep the mortar from sticking well. Set tiles briefly in a bucket of water before installing them.

10 Tip up the float, and use it to scrape away most of the excess grout. Hold the float at an angle to the tiles as you work so that it doesn't dig into the grout lines.

11 Wet a large towel; then gently drag it across the tile surface to remove most of the grout. If the towel is not picking up much grout, it may need to be wetter; but don't make it so wet that it creates pools of water.

7 If the tiles are fairly straight and the mortar bed is thick, you may be able to simply set them in the mortar. More likely, you will need to back-butter each tile to achieve the right thickness. Some tiles may need more mortar than others.

8 After filling each grid, lean or stand back to examine the layout. Adjust tile positions to make for grout lines that are consistent in width and tile lines that are as straight as possible.

9 Wait one or two days for the mortar to harden before walking on the tiles. Mix a batch of sanded grout; wait 10 minutes; then stir again. Use a grout float to push the grout into the joints, holding the float nearly flat and moving it in several directions at each point.

12 Fill a large bucket with water for repeatedly rinsing a large tiling sponge. Dampen the sponge just enough so that it picks up the surface grout, and wipe the surface gently to clean the tiles. You will need to repeat this several times.

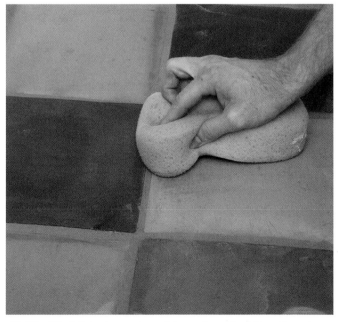

13 Wad the sponge up a bit, and run it along grout lines. Work to make the lines of consistent depth. If a gap in the grout occurs, use your finger to fill it; then wipe again.

Vinyl Composition Tiles

Vinyl composition tile (VCT) offers a low-cost flooring that is durable as long as it is protected with sealer every once in a while. Also called "commercial" tile, drab versions are often seen on the floors of grocery stores, hospitals, and schools, where they are chosen because of low cost and their ability to hide dirt. But vinyl composition has a sunnier side: many are available in bright, cheery colors and can be mixed and matched in any pattern you choose. In addition to the bright-colored standard tiles with their familiar dirt-hiding patterns, some companies carry "luxury vinyl tile" (LVT) lines with solid colors or more decorative patterns.

The subfloor should be reasonably level and even, but it need not be rock-solid, because these tiles can flex. See pages 206–7 and 212–13 for preparing the floor and laying out for tiles. The top layer of underlayment must be very smooth because even small imperfections will show through the tiles.

This arresting checkerboard floor, below, is made with 16-in.-sq. vinyl tiles in solid black and white.

The appearance of wood strips and ceramic tile, opposite, is created by using an artistic combination of vinyl tiles and vinyl sheet flooring.

TIP

Alternating or Straight Orientations

Most vinyl composition tiles have a pattern that moves in a single direction. Classically, the tiles are installed in an alternating pattern, with adjacent tiles perpendicular to each other. But you may choose to install with all the tiles pointing in the same direction.

Installing Vinyl Composition TIles

• ¼ in. luan or other plywood underlayment • Measuring tape • Power saw • Hammer (and/or air-powered stapler) and utility knife
• Wood-floor patching compound • Small-notched trowel • Sanding block • Chalk-line box • Vinyl composition tiles • Vinyl tile adhesive

1 Cut pieces of ¼-in. plywood underlayment, and arrange them on the subfloor. Stagger the seams as shown in the inset. Attach the underlayment by driving staples in a 6-in. grid. Or hand-drive flooring nails.

2 Feel with your hand and scrape with the flat side of a trowel to discover any fastener heads that protrude up. Even small bumps will telegraph through the tiles, so knock them down with a hammer.

Continued on next page

Installing Vinyl Composition TIles, cont'd.

3 Using the flat side of a trowel, apply wood-floor patching compound to the joints, fastener holes, and any other depressions. Scrape lightly; it's OK if the patch is a bit high.

4 Allow the compound to dry; then sand the floor with a hand sander. Feel with your hand as you work; many bumps and divots are hard to see. Vacuum the floor; then wipe it with a damp rag to remove dust.

5 Following the layout principles on page 213, snap layout lines. Important: the lines must intersect at a point where you will be able to reach without kneeling on the floor because you cannot kneel on the adhesive.

8 Continue laying tiles. Before you kneel onto installed tiles, press down on them firmly with your hand to completely attach them; otherwise, they may slide slightly as you work.

9 Most cut tile ends will be covered by molding, so the tiles can be cut a little short. Measure using a measuring tape for cutting a number of tiles. Try to use a different-colored tile as a cutting guide, and score a cut line using a utility knife.

6 Spread vinyl-tile adhesive using a trowel with very small notches. (A drawing on the adhesive container will show you the correct notch size.) Start at the least accessible point, and work toward where you will start laying the tiles. Use wide, sweeping strokes, and scrape up any globs.

7 Allow the adhesive to dry so it is tacky, and not wet. It will be translucent, so you will be able to see the layout lines. Carefully set the first tiles against the intersection of the layout lines. Don't press down yet; once you do, it is nearly impossible to adjust the position. Place each tile tightly against an installed tile; then lower it into position.

10 Once scored, the tile easily snaps apart using your hands. As you cut more tiles, maintain the pattern orientation (either alternating or same direction, depending on your choice.)

11 Once all of the tiles have been laid, walk over the floor to completely embed the tiles in adhesive. Use a mineral-sprits-dampened rag to clean away any squeezed-out adhesive. Apply two or more coats of acrylic or other flooring sealer.

Laying Tiles in a Pattern

If you will be installing a planned pattern, it's easy to lose track of which color goes where while you are in the midst of the installation. Use colored pencils and graph paper to make a drawing that shows where each tile will go, and consult it constantly as you work. Better yet, have a helper hand you the tiles while he or she is looking at the tiles.

Glossary

Accent lighting: Lighting that illuminates a particular area or object.

Ambient lighting: Lighting that illuminates an area or an entire room.

Backsplash: Either (A) a short (usually about 4-in.) strip of wood or tile that rests on top of the countertop at the wall or (B) the wall area between a countertop and the bottom of wall cabinets.

Base cabinet: A cabinet that rests on the floor and supports a countertop.

Building codes: The legal standards and methods that must be followed, especially for plumbing and wiring. Local building departments have their own specific codes.

Caulk (or caulking): A compound used to fill cracks and seams; it usually comes in tubes that fit into a caulk gun for easy application.

Chalk-line box (or chalk box): A tool used to mark a straight line. The line, or string, is wound inside a housing that is filled with colored chalk; when you pull the string from the housing, the chalk sticks to it. You then stretch the string taut between two points and snap it to make a straight line.

Circuit: The electrical path that connects one or more receptacles (outlets), lighting fixtures, and/or appliances to a single circuit breaker.

Circuit breaker: A device that opens an electrical circuit (shuts off the power) when demand exceeds safe limits.

Coped joint: The point at which two pieces of molding are joined by cutting the end of one with a coping saw to fit over the contours of the other.

Countertop: The work surface of a counter, usually 36 inches above the floor. Common countertop materials include plastic laminate, ceramic tile, granite or quartzite slab, and solid surfacing.

Cove lights: Lights that are hidden, often on top of wall cabinets, and reflect upward.

Crown molding: A decorative molding often installed where the wall and ceiling meet; it can also be installed at the top of wall cabinets.

Drywall: Sheets of gypsum sandwiched between backing paper and a smooth-finish front surface paper and applied to wall framing to form wall surfaces. (Also Sheetrock or wallboard.)

Dry run: The process of temporarily arranging tiles or other elements to check the layout before applying adhesive.

Duct: A passageway made of sheet-metal or plastic-and-wire tubing that carries air from a vent fan to the outside. (Also ductwork.)

DWV (drain-waste-vent): In plumbing, the system of pipes and fittings that carries away wastewater.

Escutcheon: A decorative plate that covers a hole in the wall around pipes.

European cabinets: See *frameless cabinets*.

Fixture shutoff valve: See *stop valve*.

Floating floor: A floor made of tongue-and-groove strips, sometimes glued together but not always, that rests on top of a foam underlayment and is not attached to the subfloor.

Framed cabinets: Cabinets with a face frame, usually made of 1-by strips, across the face of the cabinet box.

Frameless cabinets: Cabinets made without a face frame. (Also European cabinets)

General lighting: Light that illuminates an entire room.

Ground: The connection between electrical circuits and equipment and the earth. This may be achieved by a separate grounding wire or by metal sheathing or conduit.

GFCI (ground-fault circuit interrupter): An electrical receptacle (outlet) or circuit breaker that shuts down when it senses even a tiny discrepancy in electrical current. GFCIs are required by code in areas subject to dampness, such as kitchens.

Grout: A binder and filler applied in the joints between ceramic or stone tile.

Grout float: A flat, rubber-faced tool used to apply grout.

Island: A base cabinet and countertop unit that stands independent from walls, so there is access from all four sides.

Jamb: The vertical (side) and horizontal (top) pieces that cover the wall thickness in a door or window opening.

Joint compound: The plaster-like material used to fill indentations and holes in a drywall wall.

Joist: A framing member, usually a 2-by, that supports a floor or ceiling. Joists are usually installed 16 inches on center.

Knockdown cabinets: Cabinets that are shipped flat and assembled on the building site.

Lazy Susan: A round shelf that revolves.

Mastic (organic mastic): A ready-mix adhesive used for applying tiles to a wall; sometimes also used for floor tiles.

P-trap: A curved part of a fixture drain, usually shaped like a sideways "P," that fills with water to create a seal to prevent gases from coming into a house's interior. (Also trap.)

Pantry: A storage room or large cabinet for storing packaged foods and staples.

Plastic laminate: An impervious material made from melamine that comes in sheets and is used for the finish surfaces of countertops, cabinets, and flooring. Sometimes called by the trade name Formica.

Range hood: A ventilator fan set above a cooktop or the burners of a range. Most range hoods also include a light.

Recessed canister lighting: Light fixtures that are installed into ceilings, soffits, or cabinets and are flush with the surrounding area.

Refacing: Covering the face frame of cabinets, and either covering or replacing the faces of drawer fronts and doors.

Resilient flooring: Floor coverings made of flexible materials such as vinyl, rubber, cork, or linoleum. Wood flooring is sometimes also considered resilient.

Roughing in: The installation of the water-supply and DWV pipes before the fixtures are put in place.

Sconce: A light fixture that is mounted on a wall.

Sheetrock: A trade name. See *drywall*.

Shutoff valve: A device set into a water line to allow for interruption of the flow of water.

Soil stack: The main vertical pipe in a house that carries waste to the sewer line. (Also vent stack.)

Stop valve (fixture shutoff valve): A shutoff valve that controls water supplying a single fixture. It is usually accessible from inside a room, and there is one for hot water and one for cold water. See also *shutoff valve*.

Studs: Vertical members of a framed wall, usually 2x4s or 2x6s installed every 16 inches.

Subfloor: The supporting surface below a finished floor. In newer homes, the subfloor is usually made of plywood; in older homes it is usually made of planks.

Supply tube: A flexible tube, often covered with braided metal, that makes the connection between the stop valve and a faucet's or toilet's inlet. Supply tubes are not allowed inside walls—only where they are visible and easily reached.

Taping knife: A flat-bladed tool with a handle that comes in various widths and is used to apply joint compound or spackle to a wall.

Thinset: A cement-based mortar adhesive applied to a floor or wall for setting tile.

Tongue-and-groove: Boards milled with a protruding tongue on one edge and a slot on the other, so they fit snugly and firmly together when installed side by side.

Trap: See *P-trap*.

Trowel: A flat tool, like a small metal sheet, with a handle used for applying mortar and other adhesives. A notched trowel has teeth that produce a series of evenly spaced ridges.

Vent stack: See *soil stack*.

Wallboard: See *drywall*.

Wire connector: A small plastic cap with a threaded female portion inside, used to connect two or more wires together and to protect them from contact with metal surfaces.

Index

Resource Guide

The following list of manufacturers and associations is meant to be a general guide to additional industry and product-related sources. It is not intended as a listing of products and manufacturers represented by the photographs in this book.

American Olean
www.americanolean.com
(888)268-8453
Dallas, TX
Ceramic tile for floors, walls, and countertops; design tools on the company's Web site

American Standard
www.americanstandard.com
(800)442-1902
Piscataway, NJ
Kitchen sinks, faucets, and accessories

Arizona Tile
www.arizonatile.com
(480)893-9393
Tempe, AZ
Tile and natural stone products

Armstrong
www.armstrong.com
(717)397-0611
Lancaster, PA
Hardwood, laminate, and vinyl flooring, cabinets, and ceilings

Behr Process Corporation (a Masco company)
www.behr.com
(877)237-6158
Santa Ana, CA
Interior and exterior paint products

Belkin International, Inc.
www.belkin.com
(800)223-5546
Playa Vista, CA
Networking and entertainment products, including iPod and iPad accessories

Blanco America, Inc.
www.blancoamerica.com
(888)668-6201
Lumberton, NJ
A variety of sinks and faucets

Blum, Inc.
www.blum.com
(800)438-6788
Stanley, NC
Products for improving kitchen organization and motion, including hinges, drawer slides, and door lifts

John Boos & Co.
www.johnboos.com
(888)431-2667
Effingham, IL
Butcher block and stainless steel gourmet foodservice products

Broan-NuTone LLC
www.broan.com
(800)558-1711
Hartford, WI
Ventilation products such as range hoods, ventilation fans, and indoor-air-quality products, trash compactors, and speakers

Bornholm Kitchen
www.bornholmkitchen.com
(631)754-0464
Sag Harbor, NY
Scandanavian kitchen furnishings and design

Capital-Cooking Equipment
www.capital-cooking.com
(866) 402-4600
Santa Fe Springs, CA
Ranges, ovens, and warming drawers

Color Concept Theory, LLC
www.colorconcepttheory.com
(203) 826-9874
Bethel, CT
Interior design

Craft-Art Company
www.craft-art.com
(404)352-5625
Atlanta, GA

Specialty home surfaces, including wood, butcherblock, stainless-steel, copper, zinc, bronze, and glass islands and countertop surfaces

Crate and Barrel
www.crateandbarrel.com
(800)967-6696
Northbrook, IL
Housewares, furniture, and home accessories

Dal-Tile Corporation
www.daltile.com
(214)398-1411
Dallas, TX
A variety of tiles for floors, walls, and counters, including porcelain, quarry, terrazzo, ceramic, mosaic, recycled tiles, as well as glass and metal accent tiles

Delta Faucet Company
www.deltafaucetcompany.com
(800)345-3358
Indianapolis, IN
Kitchen faucets and accessories

DuPont
www.dupont.com
Wilmington, DE
Corian solid surface and Zodiaq quartz surface countertops, laminate flooring

The Dutch Boy Group
www.dutchboy.com
(888)521-0199
Cleveland, OH
Interior and exterior paint products, including primers, ceiling paints, porch and floor paint, and faux finishes

Expanko, Inc.
www.expanko.com
(800)345-6202
Exton, PA
Resilient cork and recycled rubber flooring, and floating floor products

Forbo Flooring NA
www.forboflooringna.com
(570)450-0301
Hazelton, PA
Linoleum floor coverings, vinyl and textile floor coverings, and entrance system solutions

Great Useful Stuff
www.greatusefulstuff.com
(800)341-9159
San Francisco, CA
Online boutique retailer of home and lifestyle products

Grohe America, Inc.
www.grohe.com/us
(630)582-7711
Bloomingdale, IL
Kitchen faucets and accessories

Grothouse Lumber Company
www.glumber.com
(877)268-5412
Germansville, PA
Wood-surface countertops and tables

Ikea
www.ikea.com
(800)434-4532
Conshohocken, PA
A range of kitchen products—from big things like cabinets and appliances to details like drawer organizers and flexible furniture

Intertile Distributors, Inc.
www.intertile.com
(510)351-3000
San Leandro, CA
Natural stone survaces

Italian Tile New York City
www.italiantilenyc.com
(718)336-8453
Brooklyn, NY
Tile distributor, specializing in imported tiles

Karran USA
www.karran.com
(866)452-7726
Vincennes, IN
A variety of sinks

Knape & Vogt Mfg. Company
www.knapeandvogt.com
(800)253-1561
Grand Rapids, MI
Specialty hardware and storage products, including drawer slides and shelving units

Kohler
www.kohler.com
(800)456-4537
Kohler, WI
A variety of sinks, faucets, and sink accessories

Kraftmaid
www.kraftmaid.com
(888)562-7744
Ann Arbor, MI
Semi-custom cabinetry with a wide selection of door styles and finishes

LBL Lighting
www.lbllighting.com
(800)323-3226
Skokie, IL
A variety of lighting products

Masterbrand Cabinets, Inc.
www.masterbrand.com
(812)482-2527
Jasper, IN
Custom and semi-custom wood cabinetry—including maple, oak, birch, cherry, and other fine woods—as well as laminate-finished products; brands include Aristokraft, Decorá, Diamond, Kemper, and Schrock

Merillat
www.merillat.com
(866)850-8557
Adrian, Michigan

Cabinetry, including accessories and storage solutions

Moen
www.moen.com
(800)289-6636
North Olmsted, OH
Sinks, faucets, and accessories, including filtration products

Oenophilia
www.oenophilia.com
(800)899-6366
Hillsborough, NC
An array of products to enhance the enjoyment of wine

Porcher
www.porcher-us.com
(800)359-3261
Piscataway, NJ
Kitchen sinks

Quoizel, Inc.
www.quoizel.com
(631)273-2700
Goose Creek, SC
Decorative lighting and home accessories

Rev-a-Shelf
www.rev-a-shelf.com
(800)626-1126
Jeffersontown, KY
Cabinet organization products

Rockler Companies, Inc.
www.rockler.com
(800)279-4441
Medina, MN
Woodworking and hardware products

Rust-Oleum Corporation
www.rustoleum.com
(800)323-3584
Vernon Hills, IL
Protective paints and coatings as well as decorative paints

Sanus (Milestone AV Technologies)
www.sanus.com
(800)359-5520
Eden Prairie, MN
TV wall mounts, AV furniture, speaker stands, AV racks and accessories

Nuvo Lighting (Satco Products)
www.nuvolighting.com
(631)243-2022
Brentwood, NY
Energy-efficient light bulbs, electrical accessories, lighting hardware, and glassware

Schluter-Systems L.P.
www.schluter.com
(800)472-4588
Plattsburgh, NY
Metal edge protection for tile installations for walls, countertops, floors, and stairs

Silestone
www.silestoneusa.com
(866)268-6837
Stafford, TX
Quartz countertops in a wide variety of colors and patterns

spiderArm Ltd.
www.spiderarm.com
iPad accessories

Stone Tile Depot
www.stonetiledepot.com
(800)622-8708
Carlstadt, NJ
Natural stone, man-made stone and tile

Sun Valley Bronze
www.sunvalleybronze.com
(866)788.3631
Hailey, ID
Handcrafted bronze hardware

Tech Lighting
www.techlighting.com
(800)522.5315

Skokie, IL
Low-voltage lighting systems and light fixtures, including globes made from blown glass

Vance Industries, Inc.
www.vanceind.com
(847)983-0960
Niles, IL
Tempered glass surface savers, wood and poly cutting boards, drawer and cabinet organizers, sink installation products

Walker Zanger
www.walkerzanger.com
(818)252-4000
Sylmar, CA
Tiles of all kinds, including mosaic, decorative stone, rustic stone, glass, metal, terra-cotta, ceramic, and porcelain

West by Southwest
www.westbysouthwestdecor.com
(800)351-6790
Lawton, OK
Home furnishings with a Southwest theme

Westbrass
www.westbrass.com
(213) 627-8441
Los Angeles, CA
Decorative plumbing

Wilsonart International
www.wilsonart.com
(800)433-3222
Temple, TX
Laminate and solid-surface countertops, including custom edges and integrated sinks

Credits

Page 1: courtesy of Behr Process Corporation Page 2: iStock Page 7: courtesy of Quality Cabinets Page 8: Dreamstime Page 9: *top*, courtesy of Kraftmaid; *bottom*, courtesy of Kohler Pages 10–11: courtesy of Ikea Page 12: *left*, courtesy of West by Southwest; *right*, Dreamstime Page 13: *top left*, courtesy of Merillat; *top right*, courtesy of Merillat; *bottom left*, courtesy of Sheri Ross; *bottom right*, courtesy of Dal-Tile Page 14: courtesy of Quality Cabinets Page 15: *top*, courtesy of Susan Serra, Bornholm Kitchen; *bottom*, courtesy of Kraftmaid Page 16: courtesy of Ikea Page 17: *top left*, courtesy of Armstrong; *top right*, courtesy of Merillat; *center left*, courtesy of Merillat; *center*, courtesy of Merillat; *center right*, courtesy of Merillat; *bottom right*, courtesy of Kraftmaid Page 18: *top*, courtesy of Ikea; *bottom*, courtesy of Quality Cabinets Page 19: *top*, courtesy of Susan Serra, Bornholm Kitchen; *bottom*, courtesy of Kraftmaid Page 20: *top*, courtesy of Forbo Flooring Systems; *center*, courtesy of Kraftmaid; *bottom*, courtesy of Armstrong Page 21: courtesy of Crate and Barrel Page 22: *left*, courtesy of Susan Serra, Bornholm Kitchen; *top right*, courtesy of Kraftmaid; *bottom right*, courtesy of Armstrong Page 23: courtesy of Ikea Page 24: *top right*, courtesy of Merillat; *center*, courtesy of Blum, Inc.; *bottom left*, courtesy of Merillat; *bottom center*, courtesy of Kohler; *bottom right*, courtesy of Oenophilia Page 25: *top left*, Dreamstime; *top right*, Dreamstime; *bottom*, courtesy of Merillat Page 26: courtesy of Grothouse Lumber Company Page 27: courtesy of Ikea Page 28: *left*, courtesy of Kraftmaid; *right*, Dreamstime Page 29: courtesy of Kraftmaid Pages 30–31: courtesy of Quality Cabinets Page 32: *top collage*, courtesy of Kraftmaid; *bottom left*, courtesy of Merillat; *bottom right*, courtesy of Quality Cabinets Page 33: *top*, courtesy of Sun Valley Bronze Page 36: *top*, courtesy of Dal-Tile; *bottom left*, courtesy of Kraftmaid; *bottom right*, courtesy of Dal-Tile Page 40: courtesy of Armstrong Page 41: *top*, courtesy of Susan Serra, Bornholm

Kitchen Page 44: *bottom left*, courtesy of Sun Valley Bronze ; *bottom right*, courtesy of Quality Cabinets Page 49: *top*, courtesy of Quality Cabinets; *bottom*, courtesy of Quality Cabinets Pages 50–51 all: Freeze Frame/CH Page 53 *bottom right*, courtesy of Blum, Inc. Page 54: *left*, courtesy of Rockler Companies, Inc. Page 55: *top*, Neal Barrett/CH; *bottom*, courtesy of Merillat Page 56 all: Neal Barrett/CH Page 57: *top*, courtesy of Crate and Barrel; *bottom left*, courtesy of Kraftmaid; *bottom right*, courtesy of Quality Cabinets Pages 58–59 all: Freeze Frame/CH Page 59: *bottom right*, courtesy of Craft-Art Company Pages 60–62: courtesy of Blum, Inc. Page 62: *left*, courtesy of Rev-a-Shelf; *bottom right*, courtesy of Blum, Inc. Page 63: top left, courtesy of Rev-a-Shelf; *top right*, courtesy of Masterbrand Cabinets, Inc.; *bottom left*, courtesy of Blum, Inc.; *bottom right*, courtesy of Rev-a-Shelf Page 64: *left*, courtesy of Kraftmaid; *top right*, courtesy of Quality Cabinets; *bottom right*, courtesy of Knape and Vogt Mfg. Company Page 65: *top left*, courtesy of Merillat; *top right*, courtesy of Merillat; *bottom left*, courtesy of Kraftmaid; *bottom right*, courtesy of Kraftmaid Page 66: *top*, courtesy of Rev-a-Shelf Page 67: *top left*, courtesy of Kraftmaid; *top right*, courtesy of Rev-a-Shelf; *bottom left*, courtesy of Kraftmaid; *bottom right*, courtesy of Rev-a-Shelf Page 68: courtesy of Kraftmaid Page 69: *top left*, courtesy of Rev-a-Shelf; *top right*, courtesy of Rev-a-Shelf; *center left*, courtesy of Merillat; *center right*, courtesy of Rev-a-Shelf; *bottom*, courtesy of Masterbrand Cabinets, Inc. Page 70: *top right*, courtesy of Rev-a-Shelf; *center left*, courtesy of Kraftmaid; *bottom left*, courtesy of Rev-a-Shelf; *bottom right*, courtesy of Knape and Vogt Mfg. Company Page 72: *top*, courtesy of Kraftmaid Page 73: *top*, courtesy of Masterbrand Cabinets, Inc.; *bottom left*, courtesy of Rev-a-Shelf; *bottom right*, courtesy of Merillat Page 75: *top right*, courtesy of Kraftmaid; *center left*, courtesy of Rev-a-Shelf; *center*, courtesy of Rev-a-Shelf; *center right*,

courtesy of Rev-a-Shelf; *bottom left*, courtesy of Kraftmaid Page 76: *top left*, courtesy of Rev-a-Shelf; *top right*, courtesy of Rev-a-Shelf; *bottom left*, courtesy of Merillat; *bottom right*, courtesy of Rev-a-Shelf Page 77: *top left*, courtesy of Merillat; *top center*, courtesy of Rev-a-Shelf; *top right*, courtesy of Kraftmaid; *bottom left*, courtesy of Masterbrand Cabinets, Inc.; *bottom right*, courtesy of Masterbrand Cabinets, Inc. Page 78: *bottom left*, Dreamstime Page 80: *top*, courtesy of Ikea Page 81: *top left*, courtesy of Dal-Tile; *top right*, Dreamstime; *bottom left*, courtesy of Ikea; *bottom right*, courtesy of Ikea Page 82: *bottom left*, courtesy of Merillat; *top right*, courtesy of Kraftmaid; *bottom right*, courtesy of Rev-a-Shelf Page 84: *top right*, courtesy of Moen; *bottom left*, courtesy of Armstrong Page 85: courtesy of Dal-Tile Page 88: *bottom left*, courtesy of Kraftmaid; *bottom right*, courtesy of Merillat Page 90: *top right*, courtesy of Crate and Barrel; *bottom left*, courtesy of Merillat ; *bottom right*, courtesy of Crate and Barrel Pages 92–93: courtesy of Walker Zanger Page 94: *top*, courtesy of Armstrong; *bottom*, courtesy of Dal-Tile Page 95 all: Merle Henkenius/CH Page 96: courtesy of Ikea Page 97: *top left*, courtesy of Dal-Tile; *top right*, courtesy of Dal-Tile; *bottom left*, courtesy of Dal-Tile; *bottom right*, courtesy of Dal-Tile Page 98: courtesy of Italian Tile New York City Page 102: *right*, courtesy of Dal-Tile ; *bottom left*, Neal Barrett/CH Page 106: *top left*, courtesy of Dal-Tile; *bottom three*, John Parsekian/CH Pages 107–09: John Parsekian/CH Pages 110–11: courtesy of Kraftmaid Page 112: *bottom left*, courtesy of Intertile Distributors, Inc.; *bottom right*, courtesy of Moen Page 113: *top*, courtesy of Quality Cabinets; *bottom*, courtesy of Kraftmaid Pages 114–15: all images courtesy of Rust-Oleum Corporation Page 116: center (cutting board insert): courtesy of Vance Industries, Inc. Page 118: *top*, courtesy of Schluter-Systems L.P.; *bottom*, John Parsekian/CH Pages 119–21 all: John Parsekian/CH Page 122: *left*, courtesy of Kohler; *right*, iStock Page 123: *top*